I0831415

From the Boarding Schools

From the Boarding Schools

Apache Indian Students Speak

Arnold Krupat

UNIVERSITY OF NEBRASKA PRESS | LINCOLN

The University of Nebraska Press is part of a land-grant institution with campuses and programs on the past, present, and future homelands of the Pawnee, Ponca, Otoe-Missouria, Omaha, Dakota, Lakota, Kaw, Cheyenne, and Arapaho Peoples, as well as those of the relocated Ho-Chunk, Sac and Fox, and Iowa Peoples.

Library of Congress Cataloging-in-Publication Data
Names: Krupat, Arnold, author.
Title: From the boarding schools: Apache Indian students speak / Arnold Krupat.
Other titles: Apache Indian students speak
Description: Lincoln: University of Nebraska Press, 2023. | Includes bibliographical references and index.
Identifiers: LCCN 2022049682
ISBN 9781496234063 (hardback)
ISBN 9781496234858 (epub)
ISBN 9781496234865 (pdf)
Subjects: LCSH: Off-reservation boarding schools—United States—Biography. | Apache Indians—Biography. | Indian students—United States—Biography. | Kenoi, Sam, between 1877? and 1881–1969? | Nicholas, Dan, approximately 1875 to 1881–1969? | Natalish, Vincent, 1878?-1922. | Geronimo, 1829–1909—Friends and associates. | United States Indian School (Carlisle, Pa.)—Students—Biography. | Chilocco Indian School—Students—Biography. | Boarding school students—United States—Biography. | BISAC: SOCIAL SCIENCE / Ethnic Studies / American / Native American Studies | HISTORY / Indigenous Peoples of the Americas
Classification: LCC E97.5 .K784 2023 | DDC 371.829/97 [B]—dc23/eng/20221109
LC record available at https://lccn.loc.gov/2022049682

Set and designed in Garamond Premier Pro
by Mikala R. Kolander.

Contents

Illustrations

Preface

Although I did not know it at the time, this book began with research on Apache autobiographical narratives for an appendix to my *Changed Forever: Native American Boarding-School Literature*, vol. 1 (2018). I knew then that the anthropologist Morris Opler (1906–96), in "A Chiricahua Apache's Account of the Geronimo Campaign of 1886," had written that it had come from "a long autobiographical account" (Opler 1938, 360) he had recorded from a man named Sam Kenoi, and that a year later, Opler had published "A Description of a Tonkawa Peyote Meeting Held in 1902" (1939), a meeting that Kenoi had attended and described to Opler. But there was nothing in Opler's published work that resembled "a long autobiographical account" from Sam Kenoi.

However, an online search among Opler's papers in the Division of Rare and Manuscript Collections at Cornell University's Carl A. Kroch Library, discovered materials catalogued as "Sam Kenoi's autobiography," and I visited the Kroch Library in 2016 to see what they might be. In the Opler Papers, Collection 14-25-3238, box 36, folders 2–7, I found a manuscript of no fewer than 704 typescript pages that was indeed the autobiography of Sam Kenoi, a substantial body of work that Opler had never published. Also among the papers were items catalogued as "Dan Nicholas autobiography" (box 35, folder 15, and box 36, folder 1), and "Chiricahua biography (Charlie Smith)" (box 35, folders 7–13). I did not then know anything about Nicholas or Smith, Apache contemporaries of Kenoi, but in examining the Nicholas folders, I found another full-length autobiography in typescript, not as lengthy as Kenoi's but a substantial 208 pages nonetheless. Nor had Opler ever published this. Unfortunately, I did not then have the time to examine the Charlie Smith materials.

But as I soon learned, Smith, like Kenoi and Nicholas, was an Apache man with whom Opler, a graduate student only twenty-five years old at the time, had worked in the 1930s, at the Mescalero reservation in New Mexico, obtaining autobiographical narratives from all three.[1] While he never did publish the life histories of Kenoi and Nicholas, Opler had included autobiographical material from a consultant he called "Chris" in his *Apache Odyssey: A Journey Between Two Worlds* (2002 [1969]). "Chris," I learned, was Charlie Smith. I cannot say why Morris Opler waited more than thirty years before publishing some of his life story, or, for that matter, why he never published the life histories of Kenoi and Nicholas.

From the Kenoi and Nicholas typescripts I learned that they had attended some of the federal Indian boarding schools, my particular concern at the time, and as *Apache Odyssey* made apparent, so had "Chris" as well. But *Apache Odyssey* offered no more than a few widely scattered pages describing his time at those schools, and I wondered whether the materials catalogued as "Chiricahua biography (Charlie Smith)" among Opler's papers in the Kroch Library might contain a good deal more about Smith's time at the boarding schools than had been included in *Apache Odyssey*. I planned to return to Cornell to find out. But at this point COVID intervened, making such a trip impossible. Fortunately, with the help of Peter Corina, a reference librarian at the Kroch Library, I was able to order scans of the "Chiricahua biography (Charlie Smith)"—box 35 of the Opler Papers, folders 7, 11, 12, and 13—that seemed most likely to contain Opler's manuscripts for "Chris's" narrative.

What I discovered from them, however, was that although Opler's papers contained a great deal more material on Kenoi and Nicholas than I had imagined, the "Chiricahua biography (Charlie Smith)" files contained almost nothing. Of the many scanned pages I obtained, there is no sustained narrative more than two or three pages long, and these contain either materials Opler omitted from his published work or early versions of notes and parenthetical remarks he included in it. A student of Opler's *Apache Odyssey* might find them of considerable interest, but they tell no new story about Charlie Smith's time at boarding school. I nonetheless reference Charlie Smith here and, occasionally, elsewhere, to fill out the context of Opler's interest in Native American personal narrative in the 1930s.

The lengthy, unpublished life histories of Sam Kenoi and Dan Nicholas deserve, I believe, stand-alone edited and annotated volumes. This, however, is not work I am competent to undertake. In that Kenoi and Nicholas had attended both on- and off-reservation federal Indian boarding schools at the end of the nineteenth century and the beginning of the twentieth, and in line with the work I had been engaged in for some time on boarding school literature—and Native American life-writing more generally—I hoped to publish those parts of their accounts that treated the time they were Indian students, along with extensive explanatory notes. I do that here.

Just as earlier research on the experiences of Native boarding school students had brought the unpublished Kenoi and Nicholas life histories to my attention, so too did research on the Carlisle Indian School for my recent volume, *Boarding School Voices: Carlisle Indian Students Speak* (2021), bring to my attention Vincent Natalish, a Warm Springs Apache born about 1878. In 1887 he was one of more than a hundred Apaches taken from imprisonment in Fort Marion, in Florida, to the Carlisle School by its founder and first superintendent, Captain Richard Henry Pratt. Natalish remained at Carlisle to graduate with the class of 1899. He then married, had a son, and lived in New York, where he was, for the most part, employed as a civil engineer. But Natalish was also active in working for the release of the Apaches held prisoner at Fort Sill, among whom were several of his relatives. Vincent Natalish did not, so far as I know, serve as consultant to any anthropologist, nor did he compose an autobiography. But he did keep in touch with Carlisle over the years, and the Carlisle archives contain many interesting items by and about him that have not previously been published or recently been reprinted. In the third part of this book, I present as much of Vincent Natalish's story as I have been able to discover. It is my hope that other researchers may learn more about this interesting Apache graduate of the Carlisle Indian School.

Acknowledgments

I'd like once more to thank Dr. Matthew Bokovoy and Heather Stauffer of the University of Nebraska Press for help and support with this project from start to finish. Two readers for the press made thoughtful and, in one case, substantial suggestions for revision, and this book is better for their intervention. Jim Gerencser of the Carlisle Indian School Digital Resource Center was again generous in response to all of my questions, and I thank him. Professor Anthony Webster graciously shared his knowledge of Southern Athabaskan and Apache speakers and texts, for which I am grateful. Ketina Taylor of the National Archives and Records Administration kindly sent me records from the Chilocco Indian School. Peter Corina of Cornell's Carl A. Kroch Library made and sent me scans of material the COVID pandemic prevented me from seeing in person, and I thank him for that. Staff members of Brigham Young University's Harold B. Lee Library, along with Richard Tritt of the Cumberland County Historical Society, Rachael Black and Perri Pyle of the Arizona Historical Society, and Nathan Sowry of the National Museum of the American Indian and the Smithsonian Institution all helped with the few illustrations I was able to obtain for this book, and I am grateful to them all.

Introduction

THE APACHES

The people called Apaches (they call themselves *Nde, T'Inde, Indeh*, the People) in the nineteenth century were made up of four principal bands: Chiricahua, Mescalero, Lipan, and Jicarilla—each comprising several divisions: Bedonkohe, Chihenne, Warm Springs, Mimbreno, and Nedhni among them. (These names appear in various spellings.) In 1848, at the end of the Mexican War, the United States took control of territories in what are now Arizona and New Mexico that had traditionally been home to the Apaches. This initiated a new development in the centuries-long history of the Apache people.

As American settlers penetrated the Southwest, the familiar pattern of contact, conflict, and ultimately conquest ensued. The Apache "wars" that broke out in the early 1860s abated for a time as the Americans' attention focused on Confederate troops in the Southwest during the Civil War, but conflict with the Apaches resumed and intensified after the Civil War, in the 1870s, and concluded only with the surrender of Geronimo in 1886. Geronimo's capitulation resulted in a great many Apache people—women and children, along with the many Apache scouts who had aided the government—being sent to Fort Marion, an old Spanish fortress in St. Augustine, Florida, as prisoners of war.[1] Geronimo himself and those who had fought alongside him were held at Fort Pickens, in Pensacola, Florida, four hundred miles away. A great many died in the humid and fetid conditions.

In 1887 the surviving Apaches at Fort Marion were transferred from St. Augustine to Mount Vernon Barracks in Alabama, with Geronimo and the Fort Pickens prisoners arriving the following year. They remained in Alabama until 1894, when they were moved once more, now to Fort Sill in Indian Territory, where they remained prisoners of war until 1913.[2] It was then that those who chose to do so—a majority of the Fort Sill Apaches—were permitted to leave for the Mescalero Apache reservation in New Mexico. Those who wished to remain in Oklahoma accepted land allotments outside Fort Sill the following year, the government having turned the area immediately around the Fort into an artillery range.

THE BOARDING SCHOOLS

The "Indian problem" confronting the dominant English invader-settlers of America was that Indians occupied lands the invaders wanted for themselves. From the seventeenth until near the end of the nineteenth century, there were, broadly speaking, only two solutions to this "problem": extermination or education. Extermination was costly, dangerous, and, as it seemed in time, *wrong*. Thus, as Robert Trennert put it, it seemed wiser for Americans to proceed with the assumption that "The Sword Will Give Way to the Spelling Book" (Trennert 1988, 3). Educating Native peoples—teaching them to speak English, to read and write, and to convert to one or another form of Christianity—was a strategy that might more efficiently free up Native landholdings and transform the American Indian into an Indian-American.[3]

The Carlisle Indian Industrial School, the first of the federal off-reservation boarding schools and their flagship, was established in 1879 by Civil War veteran Captain Richard Henry Pratt, who served as its superintendent until 1904. The school closed in 1918.[4] Summarized in Pratt's often-quoted remark, "Kill the Indian and save the man!"—erase Indian languages, religions, and cultures, and replace them with those of the dominant American society—Carlisle's ethnocidal program was long broadly adopted as the aim of Indian education in America. More recently, it has been trenchantly criticized and condemned as a major engine of colonial domination.

1. Apache buglers at Mount Vernon Barracks, Alabama. The two reclining are Sam Haozous and James Nicholas from Company I, 12th Infantry. Original card print by Burnitt of Mobile AL, date unknown. Courtesy of the Arizona Historical Society, George M. Wratten Collection, #53107.

In 1884 the San Carlos Apaches in Arizona Territory were ordered to send some of their children to Carlisle. A small measure of negotiation had been possible, but the parents could not, for the most part, withhold their consent. Then, in 1887, Superintendent Pratt himself went to Fort Marion, Florida, to select young people to attend Carlisle from among the Apaches held there as prisoners of war. Once more there was some latitude; for example, Ramona Chihuahua went east to Pennsylvania, while her brother, Eugene Chihuahua, who strongly wished not to go, was allowed to stay behind. But Pratt "went down the line choosing forty-nine boys and girls to return with him to Carlisle," as Jason Betzinez would recall this occasion many years later. And despite the fact that he was "twenty-seven, too old to be a school boy" (Betzinez 1988, 149), Betzinez was among those taken to Carlisle.[5] So, too, was the much younger Vincent Natalish. Years later, Sam Kenoi, more than twenty years old at the time, chose to become "a school boy," traveling from Fort

Sill in Indian Territory to Carlisle, Pennsylvania, in 1899. He had earlier been to the Chilocco Indian School, and, as we will see, he would go back west to Chilocco after leaving Carlisle.[6] Dan Nicholas spent several years at the Mission School at Fort Sill and also briefly attended both Chilocco and the Haskell Indian Institute, but not Carlisle.[7]

Betzinez, Kenoi, and Nicholas all collaborated with interested white people in composing autobiographies that included their boarding school experiences in greater (Betzinez) or lesser (Kenoi, Nicholas) detail. Other boarding school students, along with a good number of their descendants, wrote not only autobiography, but works of fiction, drama, and poetry that told of time at the Indian schools. There are a sufficient number of these texts to justify Amelia Katanski's assessment of "the ongoing centrality of the boarding-school experience to the American Indian literary tradition" (18). Regardless of whether "the boarding-school experience" is, indeed, central to that tradition as a whole, I believe it is nonetheless sufficiently important to Native American writing as to constitute a genre of its own, the genre of American Indian boarding school literature.

Thus, Francis La Flesche's *The Middle Five*, published at the turn of the twentieth century, might be considered the first novel in this genre, along with Zitkala-Sa's autobiographical fictions of the same period. Moving far forward in time, there are the important descriptions Louise Erdrich offered of some of her characters' experiences at the Catholic Indian schools in novels published in the latter part of the twentieth century. As for drama, we might note, among others, two plays by N. Scott Momaday set at boarding schools, *The Indolent Boys* and *The Moon in Two Windows* (2007). For poetry, a good place to begin would be the "Boarding School Poems" section of Robert Dale Parker's *Changing Is Not Vanishing* (2011), followed by consideration of more recent poems by Erdrich, Luci Tapahonso, and Laura Tohe, among many others. Jacqueline Emery has gathered examples of "Native American writings in the boarding school press" (2017), some of which might well be included in the genre of Native American boarding school literature. But this is no more than a cursory sketch of the fiction, poetry, and drama that make up the genre.

Meanwhile, the majority of Native American boarding school texts are autobiographies, and I turn here to the topic of Native American autobiography generally.[8]

NATIVE AMERICAN AUTOBIOGRAPHY

So far as written autobiographical discourse attributed to Native people is concerned, it may be described broadly as of two kinds. There are the narratives I have called *autobiographies by Indians*, like the brief autobiography written by Samson Occom, a Mohegan, probably in 1768 (but not published until 1982), and William Apess's *A Son of the Forest* (1831), a major text of Native American and American literature. There are as well the texts I refer to as *Indian autobiographies*, original, bicultural compositions produced by a Native person, the autobiographical subject, in conjunction with an editor and—usually—one or more interpreters. The first of these, published only a year after Apess's self-written text, is the *Life of Black Hawk* (1832), the work of the young Illinois newspaperman, John B. Patterson and Black Hawk, a Sauk and Fox leader; a hundred years later came the far better known *Black Elk Speaks*, the product of Black Elk's work with John Neihardt, poet laureate of Nebraska, along with many more.[9]

Neither of these autobiographical types is in any way traditional, although as Eva Tulene Watts's Western Apache stories make clear—more on these later—Apache people had been telling and circulating stories among themselves for generations in a variety of what may be called "local" genres.[10] But in contrast to their neighbors the Hopis and the Navajos, Apache people produced relatively few written autobiographical narratives.[11] Samuel Melville Barrett, a school superintendent in Lawton, Oklahoma Territory, obtained the permission of President Theodore Roosevelt to work with Geronimo on a life history while Geronimo was still a prisoner of war at Fort Sill; the resulting volume, *Geronimo's Story of His Life*, was published in 1906. Geronimo had not attended any of the American schools and he did not speak English. His nephew, Daklugie,[12] a former Carlisle student, served as interpreter for this project, although he was to express puzzlement as to why his uncle had wished to participate in it. Nonetheless, many years later Daklugie himself related some of his boarding school experiences to Eve Ball, who published her interpretation of what he had said in her book, *Indeh* (1988).

Ball had earlier published an Apache autobiography constructed from interviews she did with James Kaywaykla, probably born about 1878, and also for a time a Carlisle student. But although it is based on material provided by Kaywaykla, *In the Days of Victorio: Recollections of a Warm Springs Apache* (1970) is a text composed entirely by Ball, who, as we will see further, had also interviewed Sam Kenoi and Dan Nicholas. In collaboration with Colonel Wilbur S. Nye, Jason Betzinez, mentioned earlier, produced a book-length autobiography, *I Fought with Geronimo*, that first appeared in 1959 and dealt with his many years at Carlisle. And, as noted, some of the life history of Charlie Smith, identified only as Chris, appeared in Morris Opler's *Apache Odyssey* (1969). Smith had attended the reservation boarding school at Mescalero for a couple of years and later spent some five years between the Albuquerque and the Santa Fe Indian schools. But *Apache Odyssey* contains not even a full two pages of his recollections, and Opler scattered these widely throughout the book. Betzinez's detailed recollections of his lengthy time at Carlisle (1887–97) were highly laudatory of both the school and Superintendent Pratt, while Daklugie's memories of the place were largely, although not entirely, negative.[13] And Ball devoted no more than two pages of his autobiographical text to Kaywaykla's account of his time at the school.

Although a considerable number of Apache young women also attended the boarding schools, written records of their experiences are fewer even than those of the Apache young men, and their place in American Indian boarding school literature remains to be determined. In this regard I note that the Morris Opler papers contained a letter dated August 30, 1974, from Mary Stith, an editor at the University of Oklahoma Press, asking Opler for a reader's report on a manuscript called "Autobiography of a Chiricahua Woman, Narcissus Duffy Gayton, as told to Ruth Boyer," then of the Lowie Museum at Berkeley. Opler read the manuscript, and his response to it was not positive. He wrote to Stith of his particular concern that the text made it impossible to distinguish what in the narrative came from Gayton and what from Boyer. Perhaps there was a second negative reader's report as well, because the University of Oklahoma Press did not publish Boyer's manuscript in the 1970s. But it did so in 1992, when Boyer's work appeared with the title *Apache Mothers and Daughters: Four Generations of a Family*.

The 1992 publication does not, however, address the important concern Morris Opler had expressed nearly twenty years earlier; very much to the contrary. For Boyer, in *Apache Mothers and Daughters*, seems to have taken Eve Ball's 1980 *Indeh* as encouragement to enhance and elaborate her own representations of Apache women. This is to say that although the first-person monologues in *Indeh* were based upon Ball's interviews with Apache consultants, they are entirely her own compositions, employing a vocabulary, syntax, and diction those persons are very unlikely ever to have employed.[14]

In the same way, the four generations of Apache women represented in Boyer's book are not merely reconstructions based upon interviews Boyer had conducted with some of them, but, for the most part, pure inventions. The four generations of women Boyer chronicles are Dilth-cleyhen, a daughter of Victorio, whose date of birth is given as 1848; her daughter, Beshad-e, born in 1870; her granddaughter, Christine Kozine, born in 1904; and Beshad-e's great granddaughter, Narcissus Duffy, born in 1924. Boyer presents these women's words, thoughts, feelings, and actions in apparently literal detail, although she cannot for the most part have known them—Dilth-cleyhen, for example, died before Boyer was born and left no written record—and her sourcing, when it exists, is sometimes entirely inaccurate.

Boyer tells us, for example, that Beshad-e attended Carlisle. She does not specify the year she came to the school—it would seem to be 1886—although she does give the exact date of her arrival as "December eighth" (Boyer 105). There is no student file for Beshad-e in the Carlisle digital archives, and Boyer gives her source for the December date as "Ball et al. 1980, 140" (365n36). The reference is to *Indeh*, by Eve Ball with Nora Henn and Lynda Sanchez (1988). But while page 140 of that book contains a lengthy monologue Ball attributes to Daklugie, describing the first part of the train trip to Carlisle (in 1887), it makes no mention whatever of a young Apache woman named Beshad-e, and certainly gives no date for anyone's arrival at the school. Boyer then writes that upon her arrival, "Beshad-e was desolate" (105); but this is no more than her own fanciful imagining of what the young Apache woman might have felt. While oral tradition and family history make it likely that Beshad-e was indeed briefly in attendance at Carlisle—and probably unhappy to be there—Boyer's reportage of what that time was like is entirely her own invention. And Boyer puts in quotation marks conversations Beshad-e later had with her husband, conversations of which there is no record.

Boyer writes that Christine Kozine attended the Chilocco school, probably in 1910 or 1911, leaving sometime in 1913. But Kozine's name does not appear in the digitized Index of Chilocco students. In any case, in representing her apparent time at the school, Boyer again puts in quotation marks words that neither she nor Kozine's relatives can ever have heard. She does this again when describing the experiences of Kozine's daughter, Narcissus Duffy—whom she did know well—at the Mescalero boarding school, once more presenting in quotation marks conversations of which there is no record whatsoever, and attributing to Duffy thoughts she can only imagine Duffy might have had. Morris Opler's 1974 concern that it was difficult or impossible to distinguish the actual speech, thoughts, and feelings of the Apache women Boyer claims to represent from her own imaginings remains a problem in *Apache Mothers and Daughters*.

This is in no way the case for Keith Basso's work with Eva Tulene Watt in *Don't Let the Sun Step Over You: A White Mountain Apache Family Life, 1860–1975* (Watt 2004). Mrs. Watt, born in 1913, in 1997 invited Basso—whom she had known for some time—to record "a few family stories from long ago" on tape (Watt 2004, xiii). He accepted her invitation, and, he writes, when Mrs. Watt decided, five years later, "that her work was largely done, her taped collection of narratives had exceeded two hundred hours" (xiii). Basso explains that although Apache was Mrs. Watt's first language, she chose to narrate in English because the language skills of many younger Apaches were limited—

and because she hoped some non-Apaches would read her book and obtain a more accurate picture of her people (302n6). These stories were not, to use M. Eleanor Nevins's terms, merely "neutral information about the . . . Apache past," but, rather "explicitly moralizing and argumentative address . . . to the researcher and to White people more generally" (98).[15]

Basso states that the book was "prepared in close collaboration with Mrs. Watt," and that they worked together to choose what to include and how to arrange the material (302n6). He tells us that once the tapes had been transcribed, Mrs. Watt went over every page of the transcript and made minor changes. Further, "she requested that most of the narrative be read to her out loud," believing that if it sounded good it would be good to read (302n6); this reading led Mrs. Watt to make other small changes.

Eva Tulene Watt had attended the San Carlos reservation boarding school at Rice, Arizona, to which many Apache children were forcibly taken, but she says little about her time there. The time she spent at the Cibecue Indian School, Basso notes, was so unpleasant that she refused to speak about it altogether. She had rather a better experience at the St. John's Indian School and Mission, which she attended from the time she was twelve in 1925 until 1929, when she withdrew, and she offers some description of St. John's: its military organization, for example, and the usual boarding school pattern of a half a day of work and a half a day of classroom study. Basso's collaboration with Watt is exemplary, and very much a model for responsible autobiographical work with Native people. Several parts of the book she made with Basso might well be included in the genre of American Indian boarding school literature.

MORRIS OPLER'S WORK WITH APACHE CONSULTANTS

"Opler arrived on the Mescalero Apache Reservation in 1931" (Webster 2021, 480), and worked with Sam Kenoi, Dan Nicholas, and Charlie Smith, among other Apaches. Consistent with anthropological practice of the period, he seems, in Anthony Webster's phrase, to have "stood on the water's edge of Apache culture," positioning himself as an "objective observer getting the facts, but not a part of, not immersed in, the interactions between himself and his Apache consultants" (Webster 2021, 489). Insofar as he sought to elicit from them autobiographical narratives rather than—for example—mythic tales of the beginning of the world or historical tales of long ago, this ethnographic stance was perhaps less damaging than it might have been, and, again, Opler's was very much a practice consistent with the times.[16] It would not therefore have been likely that the young Morris Opler could have produced the sort of reliably accurate autobiographical text that Keith Basso's close and careful collaboration and consultation with Eva Tulene Watt in the late twentieth and early twenty-first centuries did.

Tape recorders were just beginning to come into use in the early 1930s, and I strongly believe that Opler did not use one.[17] I think it is certain that his Apache consultants, like Mrs. Watt, narrated in English, and they may also have done some writing for Opler. But if they did, that writing is not among his papers, nor do the papers contain Opler's notes from what I assume would be the many interviews he conducted with all three. I believe Opler may have discussed with them aspects of the manuscripts he was assembling—as we will see further, Opler was compiling life histories as a contribution to social *science*, not at all "boarding school literature"—and they may well have read drafts of some of his typescript. But there surely was not what Webster calls "an ethnohistory of communication" (2021, 476) at play, and it simply is not possible to say how Morris Opler arrived at the final drafts of the manuscripts he left behind.

Basso worked from a literal transcription of Mrs. Watt's taped speech, some of which was, as I have said, read back to her and on occasion altered by her slightly. Mrs. Watt spoke what William Leap has called "American Indian English," what Anthony Mattina had earlier described as "Red English . . . a pan-Indian phenomenon with various subdialects" (Mattina 1985, 9). Here is a random sample from Mrs. Watt: "People didn't drink very much in those days, but sometimes the mens wanted whiskey. They went across to the mens camp over there and got whiskey over there, moonshine. They used to be ashamed of it, though. In those days, if you seen somebody like that—drunk—you're ashamed for them. And the person who did it, he won't show his face for a long time" (Watt 2004, 102).

The speech of Sam Kenoi and Dan Nicholas as Morris Opler represents it almost never sounds like this, and that is surely because he edited their words, smoothing out idiosyncrasies or colloquialisms, as it were, in order to produce a more standardized or conventional syntax and diction than they had used. I will venture the guess that in the 1930s all three of the Apache men would have been pleased to be edited in that way. But that is speculation; again, it simply is not possible to say whether they had read Opler's final typescript and did or did not approve his editing of their speech.

More than twenty years later, Eve Ball, working with Sam Kenoi and Dan Nicholas at Mescalero, also does not seem to have used a tape recorder but, rather, took stenographic notation, and some of her stenographic notebooks are among the Eve Ball Papers at Brigham Young University. Although, as I have said, she would edit—or, indeed, entirely rewrite—her consultants' speech for her publications, the typescript transcriptions she made of her notes appear to be very close to the words her consultants actually spoke. And the English they spoke is very similar to the way in which Eva Watt spoke; I cite some of their words from Ball's transcriptions later.

What else might be said of Opler and his work with his Apache consultants in the 1930s? In his acknowledgments in *Apache Odyssey*, he thanked some of the senior scholars who had encouraged him to attend to personal narrative as relevant to ethnographic work. He names "Edward Sapir, one of my teachers in anthropology, who persuaded me that life history material could contribute not only to our knowledge of the content of culture but to our understanding of the dynamics of culture change" (n.p.). He also expresses gratitude to "Clyde Kluckhohn [who] continually prodded me to treat some of these life histories separately," an endeavor that was "encouraged by the faith of Louise and George Spindler in the experiment" (n.p.). These thanks, offered in the late 1960s, provide some of the historical and theoretical context for the work Opler had done in the 1930s.

As early as 1909, Sapir had published "A Personal Narrative of the Paiute War," an autobiographical account of a Wishram man named Louis Simpson, whom he had interviewed in 1905 through an interpreter. "The Wishram text is printed on facing pages with a free English translation, without rephrasing, cutting, or rearranging" (Brumble 1981, 128),[18] a commitment to accuracy. In the same year, Sapir published the account of a Takelma medicine woman, Frances Johnson, also printing both the original Takelma and a "free English translation" (Brumble 1981, 75). In 1930, working with Leslie Spier, he published the account of Johnny Bullheart, a Shasta-Molala man captured by Klickitat people about 1842, and sold to the Wishrams. Brumble assumes that "Bullheart spoke through an interpreter" (35). The *Annotated Bibliography* also lists several later personal narratives gathered and published by Edward Sapir, all of which Opler surely would have known.

Although Opler does not name him, it is almost certain that the life history publications of Paul Radin, from 1913 to 1926, were an influence on him. In 1913 Radin published the "Personal Reminiscences of a Winnebago Indian" in the *Journal of American Folklore*, a journal edited by his former teacher, the eminent Franz Boas, and an important—very nearly a foundational—document in what would come to be called "culture and personality" studies in anthropology. Ten years later Radin published his monumental study, *The Winnebago Tribe* as the *Thirty-seventh Annual Report of the Bureau of American Ethnology*, which contained a number of personal narratives from Winnebago consultants. This was followed in 1926 by *Crashing Thunder: The Autobiography of an American Indian*, presented as a contribution to the science of culture.[19]

Clyde Kluckhohn's early interest in the life history's value for anthropological insight, as he would have expressed it to the young Morris Opler, would culminate in Kluckhohn's "The Personal Document in Anthropological *Science*" (my emphasis), published in 1945, and thus long available to Morris Opler when he wrote in 1969. In much the same way, the Spindlers' "faith" in the use of life histories for cultural science would eventually be illustrated by their "autobiographic interviews" published in the 1950s, very much "culture and personality" studies.[20]

Having recorded autobiographies by Sam Kenoi, Dan Nicholas, and Charlie Smith while he was a graduate student in the 1930s, Opler decided to include parts of the last of these—that of "Chris"—in an ethnography of the Mescalero Apaches, a decision that may well have been spurred not only by Sapir's early work, and by Radin's, but also by the more recent work of Kluckhohn and the Spindlers. But why that work did not prompt him to publish parts of Charlie Smith's life history until thirty years later, nor ever to publish the narratives he had elicited from Kenoi and Nicholas, I once more cannot say.

In notes to the Kenoi and Nicholas autobiographies, I identify the people, places, and events they reference to the extent I can. Primary sources are: (1) National Archives and Records Administration, Fort Worth, Texas: Records of the Bureau of Indian Affairs, Record Group 75, Records of Chilocco Indian School Relating to Students. There are presently scans of Sections E59, "Register of Pupils, 1894–1908"; E60, "Descriptive Statements of Children, 1885–1902"; and E61, "Arrivals and Departure, 1897–1900." I once more thank Ms. Ketina Taylor of NARA for help in obtaining these. (2) An Index of Chilocco Indian students that is available at https://www.okhistory.org/chiloccosearch. (3) Carlisle School records, available at the Carlisle Indian School Digital Resource Center, carlisleindian.dickinson.edu/. (4) Alicia Delgadillo's *From Fort Marion to Fort Sill*, which offers biographies of all those Apaches incarcerated at Fort Marion and later brought to Fort Sill. All the material on Vincent Natalish comes from the Carlisle Indian Industrial School Digital Resource Center.

I also found among the Eve Ball Papers, in the L. Tom Perry Special Collections of the Harold B. Lee Library at Brigham Young University, materials catalogued as "Oral History of Sam Kenoi" (MSS 3096, box 6, folder 6). But, in fact, there is no "oral history" there. The folder contains most of an interview Ball did with Kenoi on October 6, 1954, along with a few pages of typed notes recording things he told her on one or another occasion. There is similarly an entry catalogued as "oral history of Dan Nicholas" (box 7, folder 13 of the Eve Ball Papers). Once more there is no "oral history" but, rather, Ball's typed and handwritten notes based on interviews she did with Nicholas at Mescalero from "1966–8," when he would have been in his late seventies or perhaps early eighties, along with some very brief narratives written by Nicholas himself. Ball may well have planned to use these materials to construct an extended "oral history of Dan Nicholas," but she did not do so before her death in 1984. I occasionally reference and quote from the Eve Ball Papers to flesh out some of what Kenoi and Nicholas told Morris Opler many years earlier, and to give some sense of their actual speech.

Finally, I reference in the endnotes *On Becoming Apache* by Harry Mithlo and Conger Beasley Jr. (2020). Although the book contains monologues by both Mithlo and Beasley, it is mainly the story of Harry Mithlo's father, Watson Mithlo, the son of Laurence Mithlo, a Chiricahua friend of Sam Kenoi and Dan Nicholas. According to his son, Watson Mithlo was born on July 4, 1886, and he was the "Last P.O.W. from Castillo de San Marcos [Fort Marion], St. Augustine, Florida" (Mithlo and Beasley 2020, 3), to die, also on the 4th of July, in 1993.[21] Harry Mithlo states: "What I tell you will be what I have been told by my father and mother and aunts, uncles, brothers, sisters, cousins, and friends. It's been given to me over the years in pieces, which I hope to put together like a mosaic, telling it in the way it was told to me" (4). He then offers first-person monologues that are presented as what his father, Watson Mithlo, said at one time or another. These monologues are not Watson Mithlo's actual words but, rather, Harry Mithlo's recollections of them, published in consultation with Beasley, a prolific author on Western history and culture. I include them because they offer valuable thoughts and opinions relevant to the times of Sam Kenoi, Dan Nicholas, and Vincent Natalish.

From the Boarding Schools

1

Sam Kenoi's School Years, as told by Himself

In his "A Chiricahua's Account of the Geronimo Campaign of 1886," Morris Opler wrote that the Apache man who had provided that account was Sam Kenoi, "a fifty-seven or fifty-eight-year-old man" (Opler 1938, 360) at the time Opler had worked with him in 1932. Kenoi confirms this as his age on the first page of his unpublished autobiography, where he states that he "was born in 1875" (Kenoi 193?, MS 1). Alicia Delgadillo gives his birthdate as "c. 1875" (Delgadillo 2013, 149), and this is roughly in accord with information from the Chilocco Indian School as well, where Kenoi's age upon his enrollment in 1896 was recorded as nineteen, which would give him a birthdate of 1877. But later, when he entered Carlisle in 1899, the student file created for him listed his age as eighteen, which would make his date of birth 1881. Eve Ball, who knew Kenoi in the 1950s, also took 1881 as his date of birth (Ball et al. 1988, 106).[1] But Sherry Robinson, who edited Ball's papers, quotes material that—mistakenly—presumes him to have been born decades earlier.[2] My guess is that the dates given by Opler and Kenoi himself, are probably more nearly correct, but that is by no means certain.

Not only are there several dates of birth for Sam Kenoi, but there are several English names for him as well. (I have found no mention of what his Apache name might have been.) He enrolled at Chilocco as Sam E. Keno, and at Carlisle as Sam Keno. But he signed his name Samuel E. Kenoi on a student survey he returned to Carlisle in 1910, and Kenoi was the name by which Morris Opler referred to him in their work together in the 1930s and in his later publications. At Fort Sill, as we will see, Dan Nicholas called him Sam Chino, and after 1913, when he left Fort Sill for the Mescalero reservation and became active in tribal affairs, he was known almost exclusively as Sam Chino. He had a son named Sam Kenoi Jr., as I learned from Professor Anthony Webster, who had met him at Mescalero (pers. comm., November 12, 2021), and another son, Wendell Chino, who was elected to many terms as Mescalero tribal chairman. Wendell's son, Mark Chino, Sam's grandson, also served as tribal chair and lives at Mescalero at the time of writing.[3] Eve Ball referenced Sam Kenoi both as Kenoi and as Sam Chino.[4] Alicia Delgadillo records him as Sam Kenoi, although she also gives "Keano, Keeno, and Keno" as alternate spellings (Delgadillo 2013, 149) of his name, with no mention of "Chino." I use Kenoi because that was Morris Opler's practice, and it is Opler's work with him that I am presenting.

But whichever name one may use, there remains the question of how or from whom he got that name. Alicia Delgadillo wrote that Kenoi "was a son of Tsaltaykoo and David Fatty" (149), although she had earlier said that Fatty was "Kenoi's (Samuel) *stepfather*" (84, my emphasis), not his biological father. In her commentary on "Sam Kenoi" based mostly on Eve Ball's work, Sherry Robinson affirms that David Fatty was Kenoi's stepfather (Robinson 2000, 106), and much later in her book claims that "Sam Chino said his father was a Chiricahua named José Mario" (250n23), a name I have found nowhere else.[5] Kenoi's mother, Tsaltaykoo, is said to have married David Fatty after her husband, Sam's father, died. That marriage would have had to have occurred before 1892, because that was the year Tsaltaykoo herself "probably died in Alabama" (Delgadillo 2013, 259). Speaking of that period to Eve Ball in 1954, Kenoi said, "My relatives were dead. . . . And I was an orphan. My father was not living; my stepfather did not like me. So I cook for myself; I pull out and go to Chilocco in 1895" (Ball 197?a).

But more than twenty years earlier, on the first page of the autobiography he had done with Morris Opler, Sam Kenoi said, "My father must be about eighty-eight now" (Kenoi 193?, MS 1).[6] That was about 1932, and it means that his father would indeed have been living at the time his mother married David Fatty and many years later as well. In fact, the first three chapters of the autobiography Kenoi produced with Opler deal with his father. They are called: "How my father got his masked dancer ceremony," "My father's curing ceremony," and "My father's curing ceremony for blindness." In those chapters, Kenoi describes in great detail how his father obtained strong healing powers,[7] reports that he had served in the 1880s as a U.S. army scout—in order to "make peace and bring [the resisting Apaches] in" (MS 2), and that he "sometimes came to Mescalero. This was before he was married" (MS 3). That would be after 1913, and surely references his father's second (or third) marriage, well after the death of his first wife—Sam's mother. I cannot resolve the apparent contradictions, and note only that for all his willingness to talk of his father, Sam Kenoi does not once give his name.[8]

Although Delgadillo refers to David Fatty both as Kenoi's father and as his stepfather, she does note that he "was raised by Carl Mangas" (Delgadillo 2013, 149)—perhaps because, as I have quoted him earlier, he believed "his stepfather," David Fatty, "did not like [him]" (in Ball et al. 1988, 16). Carl Mangas's role in young Sam Kenoi's life was confirmed to me by Michael Darrow, tribal historian of the Fort Sill Apache Tribe, who wrote, "Sam Kenoi was, I am told, raised by Carl Mangas" (pers. comm., July 28, 2021).

Although Kenoi was a southern Chiricahua Apache—of the same band as Juh,[9] an important leader, and of the better-known Geronimo—unlike a great many of his Apache contemporaries, Kenoi had a very strongly negative view of both men. In his autobiography he calls Juh "a trouble-maker, a witch, and a drunkard" (Kenoi 193?, MS 274), and refers to Geronimo, among other disparaging terms, as "nothing but an animal" (MS 275). After Geronimo's 1886 surrender, Kenoi and his family were among those sent by train from Arizona to be incarcerated at Fort Marion, Florida, and they were also among those moved to Mount Vernon Barracks in Alabama in 1887, and then to Fort Sill in Indian Territory in 1894. While in Florida, Kenoi attended St. Joseph's Academy, and he also went to school in Alabama (Delgadillo 2013, 151). He gives both 1894 and 1895 as the year he entered the Chilocco Indian School not far from Fort Sill, although the Chilocco index records his date of entry as 1896; he probably left in 1898.[10]

He then went east to school at Carlisle, enrolling, as noted, in September 1899—and, his record indicates, running away fourteen months later. Then, in 1902, he returned to Chilocco, mostly to play baseball, but also to be placed in the third grade, although he was more than twenty-one years old. He advanced rapidly to the ninth grade—that was as far as Chilocco went—and was offered a position as assistant disciplinarian at the school. He later farmed for a time, and married Anice Sakieh, also an Apache Carlisle student. With the majority of the Fort Sill Apaches they relocated to the Mescalero Apache Reservation in New Mexico in 1913, where Anice died less than a year later. In the early 1930s Sam Kenoi worked not only with Morris Opler but also with the anthropologist Harry Hoijer, to whom he narrated in Apache a number of Coyote tales and also texts called "Foolish People" stories.[11]

Woodward Skinner's *The Apache Rock Crumbles* includes a 1959 photo in which Kenoi, Charlie Smith, and Dan Nicholas may all be seen; James Kaywaykla spoke of Kenoi to Eve Ball as still alive in 1963, and it is possible that Ball interviewed him as late as 1968.[12] In her preface to Kaywaykla's autobiography, however, she wrote: "The Apaches mentioned by Kaywaykla as living died before 1970" (Kaywaykla 1970, xv). Ball gives no exact dates, as Alicia Delgadillo does not. Nor have I found the exact date of Sam Kenoi's death; 1969, perhaps.[13]

Kenoi's account of his time at boarding school covers the period roughly from 1895 to 1898 when he was first at Chilocco; 1899–1900 and his time at Carlisle; and then his return to Chilocco in 1902, for two more years. As the reader will discover, his time at these federal Indian boarding schools had almost nothing to do with what I have elsewhere called the *topoi* and *loci*, the topics and places, of daily boarding school life.[14] The academic study, the military drills, or agricultural and vocational instruction, the dormitories, dining rooms, and classrooms are described almost not at all, for all that these made up the day-to-day life of most Indian students at those schools. Similarly, Sam Kenoi says almost nothing about relations with teachers and the staff at the schools, nor, for that matter, does he mention many of his fellow students. Nonetheless, his account of the years 1895–1904 are importantly marked by his sense of himself as a Chilocco and then a Carlisle student, and his is very much a voice from the boarding schools.

Whether he is doing farm work, hopping freight trains, drinking with friends, or having sexual adventures with women; whether he is near the schools or far from them, whatever else Sam Kenoi was in those days he was also an Indian boarding school student, and his account of his experiences should certainly complicate any general sense of what Indian boarding school life was like. Following is most of what is catalogued in Cornell's Carl A. Kroch Library as in box 36, folder 4, pp. 327–83, of the Morris Opler Papers: Sam Kenoi's autobiography as prepared by Morris Opler. Some few minor omissions on my part are noted by ellipses. As I have said, Opler surely edited substantially whatever Sam Kenoi had told him and perhaps had written down, although materials to determine exactly what is Opler's and what is Kenoi's do not appear to exist. In any case, I have not altered Opler's typescript except on occasion silently to correct typos or very minor errors (e.g., "you're" instead of "your," "than" for "then").

I Go to School at Chilocco[15]

In 1895 I was home from Anadarko.[16] I stayed at Fort Sill three weeks and then was sent to Chilocco. I was to go for three years. I did stay all that time and didn't come back till 1898. I didn't have any vacation. There were all different tribes there but no Apaches, except two fellows who went with me. Three of us Apache boys went together. Guy Alonzo was one. He died. He came home the same year sick and died of consumption. Henry Yabikoli was the other. He came home with me in '98.[17] He was my good friend there. We all worked in the shoe and harness shop the first year. Then Guy died.

In 1896 when summer came I stayed on. I was working on harvest, getting fifty cents a day. Henry, Arnold Kinzuni's nephew, was there with me.[18] He always went with me.

One Saturday we went to Arkansas City, six miles away from Chilocco. We got there by hack. We had our uniforms on. I was a first sergeant and had big yellow stripes on the shoulder and on the trousers, wide yellow stripes.[19] They were too loud. I didn't like them. Henry was just a private. We were both young boys then. He was a couple of years older than I was.[20] In those days the streetcars were pulled by mules. We got on one of those mule-cars and rode downtown.

We went to a big clothing store, Newman's, I guess the name was. We had some money with us, and we bought underwear, nice pants and a shirt.

Then Henry said, "Let's go to a barber shop and get cleaned up."

So we went to a barber shop and got a bath. Then we put on our clean clothes and told the barber to cut our hair and wash it good with soap. When we got out of there we surely looked fine.[21]

We walked around a little and then we came to the same store. We had left our other clothes at the barber's. There were lots of people in that store. We had plenty of time because the next day was Sunday, and we didn't have to get back that day at all if we didn't want to.

While we were walking around there we saw two white girls, good looking girls. One of them started to talk to us, "Hello, boys," she said, "are you from Chilocco?"

Henry was bashful; he just stood there and wouldn't say anything. So I said, "Yes."

"How about going for a walk with us to the river?" she said. And she started for the door.

I could see that Henry wasn't going to do anything, so I started to follow them to the door. He was dumb, and where there's one dumb fellow and one lively one, the dumb fellow is going to follow the lively one every time. I knew if I started for the door he wasn't going to stay behind. And sure enough he came right along.

We started to walk right through the middle of town, down to the edge of town, along the Arkansas River. There are lots of willows there. It was summer and it was hot.

Pretty soon one of the girls said to the other, "Ruth, you take that boy and go for a walk. I want to talk to this boy."

The other girl tried to get Henry to walk with her, but he was bashful and wouldn't go. Then the other girl, her name was Rosalie, wanted me to walk with her.

I said to Henry in Apache, "I'm going with this girl and see what she wants. You stay right here and don't go away till I get back."

So we started off. We walked a long way, until we were far away from everything. Then we sat down.

She began talking to me. "I like Indian boys." She asked me my name and what I was doing and many other things. She began to put her arms around me, and lie down, and pull me around.

I began to get pretty scared. I was remembering what my father had told me about how women have teeth in there and how you get sick from them. I knew that the older boys did it to the girls and that soldiers did it to Indian women, but I never thought of what I'd do when my time came. Before this I paid no attention to girls. Now I didn't know what to do. I let her pull me around, but I didn't do anything myself. I felt like crying. Pretty soon she just lay on the ground and pulled her pants off. She spread her legs and said, "Get in there, Sam." But I didn't do anything.

"What's the matter with you, Sam?"

Then she began to unbutton the top of my pants and played with me. But I was limber. I couldn't get a hard on. Then somehow she got it hard enough to put in. "This way, this way," she said and motioned toward herself. I came down too hard. I never had any experience. I took it out and it was bloody. I must have ripped something in there. But it wasn't my fault. Anyway we started again. We were sweating like race horses. Somehow or other I finally came.

When we got up I went straight for the river. I took off my shoes, rolled up my pants, and waded out. I was scared still that I'd get the clap. And I washed it off out there while she stood on the bank and laughed.

On the way back I said, "Go slow." I wanted to see what Henry was doing. Sure enough, there he was doing the same thing. He was worse at it than I. Every time he'd come back, it would slip out, and he'd have to put it back in. When they saw us they stopped. The two girls began talking and laughing.

My girl said, "How did you make out?"

And the other laughed and said, "He just wore me out, but he didn't do anything." And that was true for Henry never came that night.

So we went back to town. They took us to the house of one of the girls.

"Come on in and we'll have tea and things to eat," they told us.

So we went in. They brought in the mother and father of one of the girls.

"These are two Indian boys from Chilocco," they told them.[22]

I felt so bad I could hardly stay. We wanted to get out. We were in one room, and the older people were in the other. Every once in a while the girls would look at one another and burst out laughing.

The mother would say, "What are you laughing about?"

"Aw, we're just laughing about something funny we thought of."

Pretty soon we said we had to go. We got out. The girls came with us a little way. "Come and see us again," they told us.

We told them we'd be back and that we'd do better next time. When we got away Henry said, "Let's go back to Chilocco." So we started back to Chilocco walking.

We did come back. We kept it up all summer, and we got pretty good at it too. Sometimes they'd come up to Chilocco and we'd take them out rowing. I was good at rowing then. Each Indian tribe had its own canoe at Chilocco. There was a Comanche boat with the name painted right on the side, a Sioux boat, an Apache boat, and so on. We'd take them out in our boat. Every time we were going to meet them we'd say, "Let's make it a good one this time." And I'd say to Henry, "Well, you want to keep it in this time."

In a section titled—again, almost surely by Opler—"How we lived at Fort Sill," Kenoi tells of his return to Fort Sill with his friend, Henry, "in '98," and of their work picking "grapes and peanuts" and earning "plenty of money." He also describes in some detail the animus between himself and his cousin, whom he identifies only as Regis.

[Regis] didn't like me. I had never known him much because he was never in Alabama. He had been taken right to school in Carlisle. He was a college boy and didn't like my ways.[23] Yet Regis was my mother's sister's son.

Before this I was always quiet and bashful, ashamed to go around a big crowd. Then Regis came and stayed with me and bullied me just as soon he got back to Fort Sill.[24] He'd make fun of me before everyone. He'd hit me with a rope and tell me he was doing it to toughen me up. He'd make me run. He bought whiskey and made me drink it. Before that I never touched it. There his mother would be, in the other side of the house, crying and begging him to leave me alone, crying because she had tried to bring me up right and now her own son was ruining me.[25]

I hated him as I never hated anyone before. I wished I could lick him, and I made up my mind that some day I would give it all back to him. I trained for prizefighting in the barracks. . . . I kept at it and got pretty tough.

I came back and fought Regis. We used to fight in there, wrecking everything in the place while my poor aunt stayed in the other half of the house crying. But after that Regis knew he couldn't drive me out, and he didn't bother me so much. But after that I was spoiled. I drank; I fought; I was tough. I was no longer bashful and quiet as I had been.

Regis was one of a bunch of Carlisle boys who came back to Fort Sill in 1894. David Kaje, Charlie Icti, Regis, and others came at the same time.[26] Instead of studying at Carlisle they went out and sang medicine songs. They'd get together in their rooms and sing every night while they were there. On Saturday they'd go to the Susquehana River and sing and pray.[27]

When they came back to Fort Sill they had a little society. They wore four ribbons, dark yellow and blue, pinned on with a cross. I was bunking with Regis. He tried to get me to come with them. They were singing and praying every night a little ways from our camp. He said I was wild and said other things about me, but I wouldn't go. He'd come home and stand there by the bed praying and making all sorts of motions. He'd take those ribbons off very carefully.

They stopped this about 1899 or 1900. I don't see them doing it any more. At Carlisle they all wanted to be medicine-men. One would dream something and he'd be a medicine-man. Then the next night Charlie would dream and he'd be one. They'd get together and tell their dreams.

David Kaje is religious crazy right now. He has his own medicine. He seems to be talking pretty good about God and Jesus.

Henry got sick in August and died in twelve days. He was taken to the hospital. I came there, and he was gasping for breath. I didn't know what to do. I just sat there and cried. He was not a real relative of mine or anything, but I thought of him as my own brother. The next day he died. And here he and I had already received papers so that we could go to Carlisle together.

I tried to find some other boys to go with me then, and I got Richard Inick and Tom Duffy to go and two Comanche girls, Corner Parker's daughters, too. One was Juanita and the other Laura.[28] They were very pretty girls. I danced with them at Fort Sill before we left.

At this point Opler inserted three pages (they are numbered 337A, B, and C) in which Kenoi tells of dealing with cousin Regis and his wife, a woman named Belle, who nonetheless "ran around" with "Nicholas, Dan's father" whom she "secretly married." This is a bit confusing but worth sorting out, in that James Nicholas was indeed the father of Dan Nicholas, parts of whose autobiography I consider next.

Belle Althchinny, born about 1874, was first married to a man named Seeltoe who, believing her unfaithful, shot her, intending to kill her. She recovered, and Seeltoe "committed suicide" in 1894 (Delgadillo 2013, 207). Belle remarried, and after her second husband died in 1900, she married James Nicholas, whose first wife, Elsie, Dan's mother, had also died. Delgadillo does not mention a marriage between Belle Nicholas and Regis Alchintoyah; she does say, however, that after his return from Carlisle in 1895, Regis "married a Comanche woman" (6), something Kenoi confirms elsewhere. Dan Nicholas also says that

Regis and Belle—who was Apache, not Comanche—were married, and I cannot explain the disparities in the accounts. I pick up Kenoi's story after some further rowdy adventures involving Regis, Nicholas, and Belle that I have omitted.

I Go to Carlisle

So in '98 I went to Carlisle. I got there in August.[29] They took us to the boys' quarters. They put the three of us in Company D. They took us upstairs to the bathroom and we had a good bath. Then they put uniforms on us.

A day or so later Duffy got very sick, and he was pretty sick all during the early part of September. The doctor sent him home.

There were Indians coming in from all parts of the states. They had twelve hundred students and no rooms for many of them. It was the middle of September and school had not yet started. Some were sleeping on the floor. They began shipping some of the students out into the country to work.[30]

I told Richard, "Let's go out with a group in the country."

So two weeks after Duffy left we went out. You had your choice.

In Chilocco I had been in the seventh grade. When I got to Carlisle and they asked me I said I had been in the second grade.[31]

Richard and I got separated. He was sent with another group. This bunch of fifty that I was with went through Harrisburg, then Reading, then to Philadelphia. From [t]here half of us were going towards Bristol and Trenton, New Jersey. Then we got to Tallytown, Pennsylvania.[32] Four of us boys got out there. Our country fathers were there with hacks. My country father was there.[33]

Here I interrupt Kenoi's narrative for a moment to note that more than twenty years later, in 1954, Sam Kenoi told Eve Ball of this outing experience. As noted, Ball did considerable editing of her consultants' words before publishing them, but she transcribed their words as she had taken them down in her stenographic notebooks literally. I suspect Sam Kenoi's speech in 1954 was very much like what it had been in 1932, and I reproduce here just a single paragraph to offer some idea of how he might have spoken to Morris Opler. I have corrected Ball's typos, and omitted a couple of sentences, but changed nothing else:

> I was with a Pennsylvania Dutch man when I was in Carlisle. I called them my Father and Mother and cousins. They work you, too; get you up at three thirty or four; milk ten or fifteen cows; work for fifteen dollars a month; go to school and drive back to Tullytown High School. Right across Delaware River, near Trenton, New Jersey. I learned a lot about cattle and farming. Just across from where George Washington crossed the Delaware. . . . I lived with a white family. Asa [Daklugie] and Jasper [Kanseah] would do the same; all the boys at Carlisle. (Ball 197?a)

Opler's typescript continues:

> "Which is Sam Kenoi?" he asked.
>
> "I am."
>
> "I am Charlie Hanser."[34]
>
> I had my trunk there. He loaded it on his hack. He said, "I'm your country father."
>
> I don't know where the other boys went. It was just turning dark. We drove four or five miles out in the country to a place called Penn's Manor.[35]
>
> Hanser had about five cows, and he had six big horses to work with. He had a big tobacco field, corn, oats, onions, and all kinds of vegetables. There I began to work for my schooling, for my room and board. I milked cows, fed horses, and curried them, and cleaned out stalls. Then I'd get on one of the horses and go to Tallytown to the white school.[36]
>
> And there I had a swell time with the boys. They didn't like Indians, lots of them. They'd call me all kinds of names. I had to fight nearly every day. It's just like if you had to go to Whitetail, Morris.[37] But the Indians don't do it like that. If you were over there alone they wouldn't abuse you. The Indians mind their parents better, and if someone told my parents I was abusing you, I'd get a darn

good licking and wouldn't do it again. Some of those big boys used to kick me every time I went past. But I made out. I played their games, played baseball, and got along in the end.

There's one thing I think is important. It's just like this. Ever since I was taken prisoner when I was eleven years old,[38] I have known nothing but mistreatment for the Indians. We were taken prisoners. I didn't know what was going to happen to us. I saw our women working in the fields with children on their backs. And here, after I got to Carlisle, it was still abuse. The white people talked about how they got us out of savagery, but they got us into worse, into slavery. I didn't know what education was for. White people were almost as badly off as the Indians in the line of education in those days. I just tried to learn a little more each year. I didn't know what it was for. But I could see that I was getting ahead. After I learned my a-b-c's, I wrote my own name. I said, "Here's S-a-m, Sam, it's one word, it seems." I picked up these things. I was a poor boy. I had no pencil. Everything we used in school we had to put back in the box. But I would pick up a board, or some cardboard, or some paper and write on it. There was lots of writing around my house.

It's different with our children today. I had to pick it up. My relatives were used to living in the wild way. I lived in camp, and they spoke nothing but Apache when I was little. They couldn't tell me, "Now when you meet someone you should say, 'How do you do?'" I had to pick it up.

It seems to me that if I had had a chance, if my people had lived and if I had not met Regis and other tough fellows and got in with fighting and baseball, schooling would have been my ambition. I think I could have learned a lot. Sometimes when I was small, I used to stay all day with soldiers to hear them talk and to pick up some English. Once there was a soldier carpenter who was good to me. I couldn't make him understand. So I took him to some sand and drew a wagon. Then he understood and made me a nice little wagon. I was proud of it. I played with it for three or four years. I always kept it carefully and wouldn't let other children play with it, for a wagon was hard to get in those days. I often think of that soldier who made me the wagon. This was back in 1889, in Alabama.

I used to watch the teachers write, and then I'd go out to the sand and practice making C's and learn to be a good penman. But there were foolish soldiers who told me wrong. Many of them told me swear words when I asked them what something was called.

At the country school in the east I got along all right after I whipped a few of the kid[s]. I stayed with Hanser about two years and didn't go back to Carlisle. During the summers I stayed on too, and when there was no school and I worked steadily, I got nine dollars a month. I got a dollar a week to spend. The rest was sent to Carlisle.[39]

I used to get papers from Carlisle which asked if I chewed tobacco, drank, ran around with girls. I had to fill in the answers. Then my country parents were supposed to correct it. There was all sorts of this stuff. It took all day sometimes. A good country father would write it right out.

This first country father of mine was a good one. He had a son, a big tall fellow. He went to the same school. But he couldn't fight. I had to help him out. I had a country sister, Nellie, too. I don't know whether it was a public school or high school we went to. It was a big fine school. I never knew what it was.

I lived right in there with those people and ate at the same table. The man wasn't religious, but the lady, Mrs. Hanser, prayed at the table. According to the report from Carlisle, I was supposed to go to church. But I didn't go much. The report went in just the same.

Every week I got *The Arrow*, the Carlisle paper. First they called it *The Indian Helper*. Sometimes I saw my report in there.[40] Every summer a man came to inspect the home. He was sent from Carlisle.

The Delaware River was between Pennsylvania and New Jersey. Right on the other side some Indian girls were working. One was a Chippewa and one an Oneida. Lizzy Chab was the Chippewa. Charlotte Bigtree was the Oneida. Very pretty girls they were too. I fought over that C[h]arlotte right in school. There was another girl there called Mary Mackay. Gosh, they were just like white girls, all three![41]

The white boys never let the Indian go anywhere in that country. If I went to see another Indian boy six miles away, I had to go through white boy country and they would take after me and fight. So I wore a sling. I used it as a belt. I was a pretty good hand at it and could kill birds with it. Sometimes I hit them while they were flying. I carried two or three rocks in my pocket all the time.

This time I was going to see Alex, an Oneida boy from New York State. The white boys saw me and took after me. We were in among some cherry trees and they began to throw rocks at me. I made for a rock pile. There were three of these boys. I hit one in the leg. He fell and was there crying. I came up to him and said, "Are you going to leave me alone?" He promised that he would, and I went on.

I met my friend. Pretty soon we came on these white boys again. They were looking for trouble. This Oneida couldn't use a sling. It was dangerous when he tried. He couldn't control it so the rocks went anywhere. So I had to fight it out with the white boys. I sent some rocks pretty close to them. Then they stayed out of range and just called us names.

After these two years with Hanser I wanted to go back to Carlisle. But instead they sent me to a place near Trenton.[42] I got a very mean country father this time. His name was Newt Ely. Mrs. Ely's aunt was a principal in Carlisle six miles above Trenton.[43]

Ely worked me plenty! Two different times he kicked me. I had eleven cows to milk, a bull to take care of, six horses to curry and feed. I slept up in an attic. At three in the morning he took a stick and hit the ceiling, calling, "Hey, come down." Sometimes he would come up and say, "Are you up?"

"Yes, sir." You had to answer him politely. If he had to call the second time he'd kick you out of bed.

In the morning I had to build a fire in the kitchen, get the milk buckets, go to the barn, feed the cows and horses, curry the horses while they were eating, and then start to milk. It was before daylight; I had to carry a lantern around. Most farmers hire someone extra in harvest time, but he wouldn't, no matter how overworked you were. And that fellow had a very nice woman and a little boy. He'd get mad at his wife all the time.

He had one hired girl, a poor girl, and he used to lick her before his wife. Once I offered to fight him because of this. He hit her with a broomstick. I jumped on him, and his wife came in crying so I stopped. The girl was poor. She was only getting about two dollars a week and board. She threatened to run away, and they watched her pretty closely, and she couldn't. I don't know what kind of law these people had. I didn't know any better myself.

Well, I'd get through milking about breakfast time. Then I had to separate the milk.[44] While I was doing it they'd call me in to eat. After I ate, I went back and finished the separating. He had big farm horses. I had to curry them. It's a wonder he didn't make me curry the bull. There was no end to the work. He didn't do anything himself. He cussed at me all the time. I had to milk again at night and got through with it after supper. Sometimes I worked till nine o'clock.

I didn't stay any two months either. He started to thresh oats in fall with horses. It's the work of seven men. All he did was cut the strings of the sheaves and cuss me. I had to run up the mound, count the sheaves, regulate the horses, and spread out the straw. He kicked me once in the morning. Sweat was running down me. That afternoon I stalled on him. I couldn't stand it. We were working in a barn. He cussed me.

I said, "Look here, Mr. Ely, can't you hire another man? I'm played out."

"What did you say?"

"I'm played out."

He kicked me. It was the second time that day. When he kicked me this time I dropped that pitchfork. I picked up a wooden block, a thick piece of wood that we used for a brake. I didn't want to hit him in the head. I wanted to hit him in the arm or leg. He ran for the house. I tried to make him fight. The horses were still going. He wouldn't fight. I chased him clean into the dining room. Then I went upstairs to the attic and dragged my trunk down. Bang, bang, bang, it came down the stairs.

I told him, "I'm going to leave." I made him give me money. He gave me twelve dollars. I told him, "I'm going to Trenton."

"The sheriff will bring you back."

Out there at the barn the horses were still going round and round.

I didn't go to Trenton. I went right along the river to Falsington, then to Tallytown. I struck one old man, George Peak, there. He was a man for whom Duncan Balachu used to work. He had pictures of Charlie Icti and Duncan in his house.[45]

"You work for me and I'll give you ten dollars a month," he said.

He treated me well. He had two daughters. I stayed there. They wrote to Carlisle for me.

Colonel Pratt wrote back: "Mr. Ely is not going to have any more Indian boys."

I never had better folks to stay with. The only thing I had to do was milk cows and drive the girls around. Both were school teachers. The school was four miles away, and I had to take them and get them. I had two cows to milk. I wiped dishes and scrubbed them. I did it on my own hock, whether they wanted me to do it or not.

I said, "I want to do it for my country mother."

In spring, when school was out, I started to do more work around there. But in fall I got uneasy again. I'd been saving money. I wrote to Carlisle in fall. I had been going to school in the day too when I took the girls down. I wrote to Carlisle and told them I wanted to come back. I did it before the people I was staying with knew it. They wrote back from Carlisle to find out why I wanted to leave. Then George Peak found out.

He asked, "Why, Sam? Stay here."

I said to him, "I've come east to go to school and here I've been in the country all the time. I want to go back and see where I'm at."

I had about thirty-five dollars in my pocket. We all went down to the station. I got to Philadelphia and changed for Harrisburg. I got back to Carlisle about nine in the evening. A street car runs right up from Carlisle Indian School to town.

I went to the disciplinarian.[46] He found me a room. New students were coming in. It was the first week in September and I was going to school at last. This was in 1900. They asked me what grade I was in. I had been in eighth grade. But I told them third grade. The next day they put me in fourth. This kept going up to grade 9-A. For two days after school started I went to study hour at night.[47] I had money in my pocket.

I run away from Carlisle

Then I got a letter from my aunt. My own sister had died, she said. Oh, but I felt badly! It was the study hour the second night that I got the news.[48] I was in my best clothes, in my band clothes, a blue uniform.[49]

When I got back from study hour it was dark as pitch. I dropped my suitcase through the window. I had overalls over my clothes. I picked up my bag below and walked to Carlisle. My heart was just crying. I was crying part of the time. I didn't know where I was going. It was just an hour from bed time, nine o'clock. Study hour closed at eight.

I walked all night. In the morning I was about two miles from Hagerstown, Maryland.[50] I had been in Carlisle only two weeks. I had only four more grades to go through to graduate when I ran away. I didn't care if I died; I didn't care what I did. You know how foolish a fellow takes it.

Here, by way of comparison, is how Sam Kenoi very briefly summarized his Carlisle experience for Eve Ball in 1954. He was in his eighties then, and he misremembers how long he was at the school (it was about fourteen months) as well as the highest grade he had attained:

> I was at Carlisle nearly five years. I went only to the tenth grade. All time going to school; working for the people in the summer and working for my board in winter. Then I take the boss's children and go to school with them. (Ball 197?a)

Six pages of the typescript now depict Kenoi's hopping freight trains west to Chicago, more or less headed back to Fort Sill. He is taken for Japanese, threatened by a gang of whites, befriended by a group of Blacks, and encounters both sympathetic and abusive railroad employees. I pick up on his arrival in Chicago.

I was in the Chicago freight yard at sunup. There was just nothing but box cars all around. I got on top of a box car. I saw nothing but box cars. It looked just like a floor. It scared the wits out of me. The tops of the cars shone all around.

A man came along with a little cart. I asked him, "What is this place?"

"Chicago."

"Which way?"

"This way."

I walked and walked all morning till I got to the big city. I met a fellow, dressed up fine.

I spoke to him, "Say, fellow, I'd like to ask you a question."

"All right."

"Are you familiar with this town? Do you know Dr. Montezuma?"[51]

"Yes. Get in this store and I'll call him."[52]

They got him on the telephone and I spoke to him. He knew who I was for he had been to see the Apache boys at Carlisle twice.[53]

As soon as he heard who I was he said, "I'll bet I know what you did." Then he said, "Wait, I'll send my man down after you."

I waited about a half an hour. People were passing, driving nice rubber-tired buggies. A fine buggy came and stopped right there. It was pulled by two fine horses, and they stood there, one with his head one way, the other looking the other way. It was Dr. Montezuma's buggy. The driver took me to Montezuma's office.

I came in and saw him. He looked like Jasper,[54] about his size and dark. He had his apron on, and people were coming in all the time. There I was, a tramp.

He told me, "Clean yourself up. I'm pretty busy right now. I'll see you in a little while."

It looked to me like a drug store. About nine o'clock he slowed down on his work and called me in his office.

He said, "They keep me pretty busy."

He taught over at a medical school and had his own business too.

"What are you doing around this part of the country?"

"I ran away."

"The best thing to do is to go back." He tried to talk me into it.

I told him why I had done it. I told him that something had come across my heart and I just wanted to go home.

He said to me, "I love all you Apache boys. I want you to be lawyers and doctors and educated men so you can help your people.[55] Have you any money?"

"No, sir, I'm broke. I've been beating my way." I had twenty-six dollars.

He opened a safe, and he gave me five five-dollar bills. "There, that ought to help you get home. What do you want to do, stay here for a few days, or go right home?"

I didn't care to stay around after I got the money, and I said, "I want to go right home."

"Well," he said, "you go to the Union depot. I'll have the same man take you in the hack."

It was a long way. If I had had to walk it, it would have taken me till dark.

Freight was going through there. I jumped on a freight. It carried me to Joliet, Illinois. I got there about three o'clock. Joliet Penitentiary is there, and just a little way from it is the city. I got off at the penitentiary. I walked up to the jail.

Kenoi visits the prison briefly, and then hops trains to Kansas City, Missouri, where he just happens to encounter a parade featuring Buffalo Bill on horseback and Indians in war bonnets. Because it is illegal for Indians to purchase alcohol in Missouri, he poses as a Mexican and does a fair amount of drinking. He once more rides freight trains, continuing almost two hundred miles west to Newton, Kansas.

I went through Florence, Kansas, Augusta, Kansas, and then Newton, Kansas. At Newton the train stopped. There was a big election meeting going on there. Maybe it was for McKinley.[56] Lots of people, whites, were going into a big hall.

Pretty soon a deputy sheriff came up to me. "Where do you come from? Are you an Indian?" he asked.

"Yes."

"Where are you from?"

"Kansas City."

"Are you a runaway boy from Haskell?"[57]

"No."

"I think you are. I'm going to keep you here till I find out."

"I've got a job ahead. If I'm not a runaway, you've got to give me a dollar for every day you keep me."

"All right. I'll put you in my home and pay you a dollar a day if you are not a runaway." In those days there was a fifty dollar reward for runaway Indian boys, and that was what he was after.

He sent telegrams to Chilocco and Haskell to see if any Indian boy of my description had just run away. He got telegrams back saying that I wasn't wanted. He didn't know anything about the Carlisle Indian School. So he paid me the three dollars and let me go.

I took a freight again. I went on to Arkansas City. I came in at dark and went to a hotel, a saloon. I found some of the Apache boys from Chilocco in town. I didn't tell them anything about what I had been doing. One asked me where I had been and I told him, "Don't ask that question. Let it alone." I went to a barber shop and had a head wash and shave and got cleaned up. We fooled around there.

The next day I went up to Chilocco school with one boy. I stayed at Chilocco about two days. The teachers asked me to enter the school again. But the boys there all knew I had gone to Carlisle, so I thought I had better get away from there before they questioned me too much.

A farmer who lived four miles out from Chilocco came through there. His name was Jim Ray. He was a wealthy farmer. He was hauling sand from Arkansas City Railroad for cement. He met me and gave me the job of hauling sand. He took my stuff to his house.

The next day I went for the sand again. It had taken me nearly two weeks to bum from Carlisle to Arkansas City. I worked several days hauling sand for him. He had no farm work to do then. I stayed home alone, milked the cow, churned, fed the horses. I stayed on and worked for him. They went away for a month a time. He gave me twenty dollars a month and board and a place to sleep.

Jim Ray was over middle age. He didn't have much sense. He was just as crazy as could be. His wife was a young woman. He liked me and so did his wife. Sometimes he went off by himself for a week, and I stayed home with the lady. He surely was funny, and he didn't care what he did right in sight of me, too. He didn't care what he said either. He was always jolly. I worked for that gentleman from September on. Every time he paid me I saved a little bit. At Christmas time I had a pretty good stake, about forty dollars.

I told him, "I'd like to go to Oklahoma City."

My intentions were to go home, but I told him I'd be back after New Year's. About two days before Christmas he took me to the railroad in a hack. I was heading for Oklahoma City, he thought. Instead of that I got to Guthrie, Oklahoma. When the train stopped at Guthrie I got off, for it was going to stay there for twenty minutes. I ate at the lunch counter at the depot.

I walked around to the telegraph office. I saw some girls in there, but I thought they were all white girls. Pretty soon one of those girls who had been typewriting looked up. She smiled. I went on and then came back. She winked.

Well, the train was almost ready to start and go to Oklahoma City. I walked on again. She smiled at me again. We were getting on too fast like. Then she came out to see where I had gone.

She came up to me. "Is that you, Sam Kenoi?"

I looked at her closely. I recognized her now. She was a Pawnee. I had gone to school with her for four years at Chilocco. She had graduated after I had left there. I hadn't known her at first, for she had changed a great deal. She was wearing gold spectacles. She didn't need them but was just wearing them. She was Gerty Esaw.[58]

She said first, "Don't you know me?" Then, "Where have you been all this time?"

"Working around."

"Where are you going?"

"Oklahoma City." And I told her, "The train is starting pretty soon."

"No, don't go. Stay here. I have a place in town."

"I'll lose the use of my ticket."

"No, you won't. Give it to me."

She went over to the office with it and got me my money. They could do that, I guess. She said, "You go up town and I'll meet you tonight at quitting time. I must go back to work now." So I fooled around there.

At quitting time I went back. You couldn't tell her from a white girl.

We dragged around and talked. I said, "Where are you staying?"

"In a hotel."

I said, "I don't know the town or a soul here but you."

We went to a restaurant where she boarded. My stuff was still back at Ray's farm.

She took me to her room. She brought out pictures. She reminded me of the time we played Juanita College at football.[59] Then I got a room on the same floor as hers. In those days rooms cost fifty cents. I used my room the first night. I studied the girl to see if she was just talking nice. I had everything on her. I had been just passing through there when she had appeared and changed my ticket and everything. We sat up there till ten o'clock, I guess. But I knew I had a whole lot of things on her. I didn't say very much. She showed me a great many pictures and talked. I didn't say much. She was doing all the talking.

I did say, "What am I going to do tomorrow?"

She said, "I'll tell the boss I've got a friend in town, and he'll let me off for the afternoon."

So that's one more thing I had on her. I studied the proposition between her and me. I lined it up good on my side.

I said, "I'll go to bed, I'm tired."

She asked me where I was working. I told her Chilocco. I didn't say anything about Carlisle.

I said, "Well, goodnight, I'm going to bed." I went to my room, undressed, and went to sleep.

I was pretty active those days, night and day. I got up at three or four in the morning and washed up and walked around. I went to the restaurant. She was still sleeping. I didn't bother her. I waited about thirty minutes. Then she got up and came to my room and said, "Are you up? Let's go down and have some breakfast."

The night before I hadn't had a very good time. After I had eaten with her that first time I forgot to go to the toilet. When I was in her room I had to go. I tried to excuse myself, and she brought up something else every time. She didn't give me a chance. I looked at the clock. I thought to myself, "If I stay here ten or fifteen minutes longer, I don't know what kind of a friend she will have." I looked at the clock. One hour, another hour went. When I got out and went to that toilet I surely held it down! When I got out I was fair-minded, light.

That second morning she went to work. I sized up the town. I didn't know a soul. I watched the clock. It was time for her to quit. I picked her up, and we ate.

"Let's go up to my room," she said.

We went up and I sat down. She began to talk. She started the same thing, asking about what people I lived with, what kind of tribes are over there, and so forth.

I said, "I'll answer some of your questions. I live in Fort Sill, and it's very dear to me, too. It's a very beautiful place. It's in the prairie country, fine lands, plenty of water, a big creek is there that you might as well call a river. There is a nice scene of a big mountain in front, beautiful. We have one big school about two miles away, a Comanche school, and we have another school on the reservation, a mission school.[60] I notice lots of Haskell students employed there."

"Oh," she said, "I wish I was there."

"I wish you were too." I started on her now. I told her of one girl, Belle Kenoi'e, who was employed there, and about another girl, a Seminole, employed there.

"Did you ever go to see them?"

"Yes."

"How are the Indians fixed there? Are they earning money? Do they raise crops?"

"Sure, they have no three story houses, they just have a little house and a barn."

"Have you got a house?"

"Yes, I have a house and a barn. I could stay there, but I've been going out. Now I am working for Mr. Ray."

"Where are you going now?"

"I intend to go home."

"Where's your trunk?"

"At Jim Ray's."

"Your ticket was bought to Oklahoma City."

She caught me there. I said, "I could have my ticket bought to Ponca City."[61] Then I asked, "How is your country?"

"Oh, the Pawnee are all singing and eating peyote, and I'm afraid of them.[62] There are a lot of witches there."

I asked her, "Do you believe in witches?"

"Sure, all the old people do."

"You must not believe in what you don't see."

"If you see it, you'll be the witch." We kidded each other like that. Then she said, "If I drop around to your reservation will you see that I get a job?"

I told her this. "I have nothing to do with those people who give jobs." I felt like saying, "If there's any job I'll get it myself."

Then she came down to it and said, "If you get married, what tribe would you marry into?"

"Well," I said, "I'll answer that question in this manner. If I was to get married, I'd use my own judgment. If I make a mistake, it's just my own mistake; but if I get married, I'm not going to go according to nationalities with the exception of negroes."

"Would you marry a Chinaman?"

"I don't see any Chinamen here. I'd marry a Japanese." We were just fooling around, doggone!

She said, "Would you marry an Osage?"

I said, "I'd marry a Pawnee if I had love for her in my heart."

"Well," she said, "that's good."

Then it was my turn to talk. I said, "You might be just the opposite of me; you might want to marry a white man."

"It's just like this. I won't marry any negro either, but I'd marry a white man or an Indian."

I said, "Let's go out." I began to have to go to the toilet. I acted like I was going to my room, but I went to unload. I came back and knocked on the door.

"Come in," she told me. I went in and she was dressing. She was in her underwear. She said, "We Indians can undress before each other. We're not like the whites."

I said, "Your people are just like mine. We're Indians."

She was coming out with it now. She was shifting me around. There were many things she had been saying that were flirting. I sized it up that I was going to get it down by the river or that night in her room.

We went down by the river. There were many willow trees there, and it was warm there. No one could see us. She had her head down, thinking, throwing something into the water now and then.

I said, "What's the matter?"

She said, "I'm thinking of something near."

I said, "I'm bashful; there's something I'm thinking too."

"Don't be bashful, Sam."

"What are you thinking?"

"I want to go to Fort Sill with you."

"What would you do there?"

"Anything you say."

"You don't mean it?"

"Yes, I'm thinking hard. I want to go with you to Fort Sill. My job doesn't amount to anything. I don't know when I'll quit, and I don't like to go back to my people."

"Well, Gerty, I surely feel sorry. Have you got money to do this with?"

"Haven't you?"

"Yes, but I have to go back and get my stuff."

"You could have it shipped. Sam, I'm going to tell you just how I feel. You think I'm kidding, don't you?"

"No, or I would have gone on."

"What you say, I believe every word of it."

"All right," I said, "we've got to come to a good understanding before we do these things. Gerty, why is it you want to go to Fort Sill?"

"Because I like you. Don't you like me?"

"Just because you like me and I like you isn't enough. Maybe you won't be able to get a job there and that won't fill you up. You come right out and tell me what you mean."

"What do you mean, Sam?"

"Now look here, Gerty, like and love are two different things. We haven't come to love yet. I know that if you didn't love me you wouldn't go to Fort Sill with me. That feeling you have is way beyond 'like.'"

"Sam, would you love me?"

"Sure, I'd love you if you'd let me."[63] I was just a bum hit up with a well educated girl. I wanted it; my pants were all wet. I wanted it ten times more than she did.

Pretty soon I pushed up to her.

She said, "Are your people mean?"

I said, "The only one I cared for died. I'm a poor boy. I have a home and horses, and I'm making a living."

"Your people might get mad at me."

"It's my own business."

"Shall we go back?"

"Well, I'll let you know before the night's over. Do you really mean you'll let me love you?"

"How do you want me to show you?"

I took her hand, and I petted her. "You're mine," I said, and she said, "You're mine." Then we rolled over and forgot all about this foolish talk.

I got all I wanted that day. She said, "I surely love you. I want you to be my husband. You can sleep with me tonight." We had had it twice already. There was nothing wrong in it. We both liked it. I took her just like my wife.

On the way back we saw some of her friends. They asked, "Well, Gerty, have a nice time?"

Afterwards she married a white man, the champion rider of Oklahoma, a little fellow. I saw her at the 101 Ranch show once.[64]

In those days having a girl was nothing to me. Fifteen minutes later I could walk as though nothing had happened. After this I acted just the same as when I first met her. She might have been thinking about it, but all I thought of was that I had some more coming. That's the way I looked at it. I've done it right here at the feast grounds many times. When I'd see the girl the next morning, I'd act as though nothing had happened and as though I had not seen that girl for a year. I figure, well, after you do it you can't put your hand in and pull it out; it's over and done. Some boys are bashful about it. They hide from the girl they have done it to, and it shows up then. But this time I talked and laughed. People thought Gerty was a good girl.

We went upstairs. She said, "Right here is where we are going to stay all night."

"Yes, I'll stay," I told her.

I had a little better than forty dollars left. I didn't know what I'd have to pay for the room then; found out later.

Pretty soon she brought in a table and some cards. She wrote her name on one of the cards. "You beat that, Sam."

They were good cards; cost ten cents a piece. I wrote her name in gold ink. It looked pretty. I wasn't shaky then. I used to draw well too. I used to draw a United States map in just a little while and could draw big eagles sitting on a rock or flying. I used to get 100 every time in drawing and writing. The only place I used to fail was arithmetic. Doggone! that was hard, but I stayed with it.

"Well, Sam, I'm going back with you. What do you say?" This was at nine o'clock.

"I'll let you know tomorrow."

"I want to know now."

"I'll let you know tonight." I was anxious to go to bed. I started for the toilet.

She said, "Where are you going? Aren't you going to be with me?"

I said, "Yes," and went right on. I heard her laugh.

She went too. I put the lamp low and put paper around it. I took the basin and washed myself. I powdered myself. "Which side do you want?"

She said, "The wall."

I put the lamp out, told her it was dangerous. We talked and had a nice time all night. She enjoyed it.

Just before we went to sleep she said, "What are you going to do?"

I told her, "I'm going to Fort Sill tomorrow. I'll leave ten dollars with you. I'll write to you and come back for you. Would that be fair enough? I'm going to rush and fix things up."

I gave her ten dollars and paid my board. My pocketbook was getting slim again. She wiped a tear off when I went.

I started for Oklahoma City. I got drunk there. I was there New Year's Day. I didn't go home. I left Gerty on Christmas day. A very nice day to leave your sweetheart! But I gave her the ten dollars so she could buy herself something because I didn't give her any present.

Kenoi remains for a time in Oklahoma City where he drinks a good deal and gets picked up at a boxing match by a married Cherokee woman who runs a brothel! He writes that he stayed with her for five days and "lied to her all the time." He also writes to Gerty and lies. Then he travels back to Jim Ray's farm and works until spring. Finally, he returns home to Fort Sill.

My father had a village by the gate, by the highway.[65] There I met them, my people. I still had my uniform on.[66] My father was under a shade with others. Some women cried, they were so glad to see me. They told me, "Your aunt died." It was bad news for me, but I couldn't help it.

I went over to my place. The shade and stable were all burned down.[67] The house was still up. I stood there weeping in the house where I was raised.

I went to my father's place but was only there three days. Then my stepmother used bad words to me, and I pulled out.[68] First I went to Hugh Chee's and stayed a little while, then to Kaitah's.[69] I stayed there. Their place was close to my house. I cleaned up around my house. There was no fence around it. I began to build one. I polished up the place and pulled the weeds. I made everything look new. I stored some food there.

It was spring. I went and began to plow around my house. I knew how to farm. I got seeds, chili, tomatoes, June corn, other corn, watermelons, cantaloupes, peas, and green beans. I went right back into my house. Many Indians wouldn't have done it.[70] I washed the place out well. I was in there by myself. I used the same cook stove that my aunt had used. It was almost in the same position. I planted in my aunt's field, and she had only been dead two months!

I had some neighbors. Dexter Loco used to live near, and James Russell, Geronimo, Perico, Old Paul, and Benedict were my neighbors.[71]

Now the rains began to come. Years before, when I was a little boy, I had bought five peach trees and had set them out just for fun.[72] Now they were big. In spring they blossomed.

I figured that if I could farm for white people I could do it for myself. I planted sweet potatoes. They grew up fine. I planted tomato seed right in my house. Then I set out the plants. I did the same with cabbage.

The June corn came up and was ripe before anyone had truck ready to sell. I was selling my corn to soldiers. I sold roasting ears to them and onions. Then came the tomatoes and chili, green chili.

Then the cabbage came along and the sweet potatoes. I had money all the time. Then the watermelons were ripe. I sold them for five and ten cents a piece. Those soldiers got to know me. I plowed up my sweet potatoes. I got along pretty well.

All this time I was sleeping in the camp where my aunt had died. The Indians would say, "Did you hear anything last night?"[73]

I'd say, "No." They were afraid of it.

Regis wasn't bothering me much now. It was the first time when I came back from Chilocco in 1898, before I went to Carlisle, that he made so much trouble for me. Then he tried to drive me out of the house. But I wouldn't go, and he finally went off to another aunt while I stayed with his mother. But I had a little trouble with him again in 1901 when I was doing all this trucking.

Regis wanted to move into my house again. He was married at the Pan-American Exposition.[74] Belle Nicholas went there as an Indian Princess, and he went as interpreter. When he got back he moved into my aunt's place and began to abuse me.

Kenoi now once more states that Belle Nicholas had become Regis's wife—whom he beats, this serving as another matter of contention between him and Kenoi. Kenoi finally drives the couple out of his house, and further describes Regis's carrying on. This is the last time Kenoi will speak of Regis. It is, however, possible to hear from him in his own words because, some ten years later, he completed and returned a questionnaire sent to him by Moses Friedman, Carlisle's third superintendent, that has been scanned in his file. I'll briefly interrupt Sam Kenoi's narrative here to offer another Apache voice from the boarding schools.

Regis Alchintoyah entered Carlisle in April 1887 and remained until November 1895, when he was allowed to return to Fort Sill. Here is what he had to say about Carlisle on a questionnaire he returned to the school dated June 4, 1911. The first question asked, "Are you married and if so to whom?" Whatever his matrimonial history might actually have been, Alchintoyah wrote, "unmarried." The last question asks: "Tell me anything else of interest connected with your life." Here is his unedited reply:

I have favor note, which has come to my hand. and was very glad indeed, and to know. that dear old Carlisle still remembers me. When have received you kindly letter. it reminds me. as though I was at Carlisle again, and have deep feeling, wishing how I could be at Carlisle. so I determine to write you, a short note to let you know how glad I was. Fort Sill reservation containing nothing but the Indian [illegible]. what they called apache cattle. we have over fifty thousand cattle here at Fort Sill reservation. we generally brand the calves every summer. and it is almost time to round up the cattle. its lot of fund, when they brand the calves, we brand every year during the fall. we ship six or seven hundred head of steers. when they get their cattle money. some of the Indians gets. eight-hundred dollars, some of them three four hundred. But I do not know where all that money go to. they do not know. how to save their money.

Yours truly.

Regis Alchintoyah

What I've taken to be periods may only be blemishes in the original or the scan, but I've put them where they seemed to me to be placed. The file can be found under Regis Alchintoyah's name among the "Student Records" gathered at the Carlisle Indian Industrial School Digital Resource Center (carlisleindian.dickinson.edu/student_records), where anyone can consult it. I suspect that Sam Kenoi's English would have been roughly comparable to Regis Alchintoyah's if it had not been edited by Morris Opler. Carlisle also has a file for Kenoi from April 1910, when he too filled out a questionnaire sent by the school. The first question asks if he is married. He answers, "Yes, To Anice Sakieh," and he says that he is again attending the Chilocco School. But he leaves most of the questions blank, including the one asking: "Tell me anything else of interest connected with your life." There is nothing else from him in his file, and I have not found any of his own writing elsewhere.[75]

Kenoi's wife, Anice Sakieh, also returned the 1910 questionnaire to Carlisle. She wrote that her "present occupation" (Question 4) was "Keeping house for myself," and in the space for answers to Question 7, "Have you been in the Indian Service? In what positions? How long in each?" she wrote, "None. Please let me know how old is the youngers Students you got in Carlisle these days?"[76] For Question 8, "What other positions have you held since leaving Carlisle?" she responded, "Work in Apache Mission here at Fort Sill O.T.[77] Cooking. I am interested in Christian life for the lovesome of my Childrens." She too leaves the ninth and last question—anything else of interest—blank.

I Return to Chilocco.

In 1902 towards spring there was a new superintendent named McGowan at Chilocco.[78] I was sent to Snyder, Oklahoma. A Mr. Hunter came to see us about horses to be driven over from Snyder to Chilocco. We were going to get a dollar a day when we got to Chilocco and some clothes, too. McGowan wrote to the captain at Fort Sill. We got in a hack. A Pueblo Indian was in there and Bruce Kaedine.[79] I didn't know when I'd get back. We went to Snyder. It took a day and a half.

The next day we were at McGowan's. While we were there a cyclone came. I was on the porch when it was sighted, and we all made for the cellar. That cyclone came down three times before we lost sight of it.

The next day the horses were brought up. They were active and restless. The ones we were to ride while driving the others were saddle-horses, but they had just been broken. We saddled up. Bruce got on one. He couldn't ride it. So I tried it. Its ears were up and its back arched. It pitched, but I rode around. I didn't let him get his head down or it would have been all off. I had him licked. I got on easy. I knew he was going to pitch. If he was going to get his head down, I was going to tie the reins to the pummel so that he couldn't do it. It was a pretty horse with long tail and mane. Some of the other horses got away. I headed them off.

We started to drive the horses. We got to Fort Sill in two days. The next day we were north of Apache. The next day we got almost to Colony. The next day we got into Colony. The trip took nine days. If it hadn't been for me, I don't think they could have got those horses to Chilocco. I tried every way to get them in.

When we got to Blackwell the Chilocco Indian baseball team was playing there.[80]

We camped at Peckham, then at Chilocco. There were a thousand students at Chilocco. There was one Montana boy, a cripple, who dressed like a cowboy all the time and wore a red shirt. He was doing a lot of riding there. And here I had no books even! We swung the horses around in the ball park just to show off. Lots of girls and boys were watching us.

McGowan said, "Boys, any of them you want to ride, you can."

We rode for almost a week. We had a rodeo every day. That Montana boy was a Crow Indian. He was the only one who rode the broncos all the time. I guess he rode all of them.

Peter Gaines was in school there, George Peso, too.[81] Peter had boots on. I never knew that he was a good rider, but he got on a horse and was riding every day. George Peso was a good rider too, but he didn't want to show them. I didn't want to go on to Ramas with the horses, so he paid me off.

Just then they were forming a league, a baseball league, and Chilocco Indian School was going to be in it. The Boston Boosters came. The superintendent was getting old students to make up the Chilocco team. He found out I was a good ball player. The old students were coming in.[82] Sam Morris, who was a pitcher for a coast league team in California came. Joe Taboo, a catcher, and Sam Horsechief, a Pawnee, and another Pawnee boy came. I had gone to school with all of them at Chilocco in 1894.[83] Tom Duffy and I were on this team. School was going on, but I didn't go to school. I had been just hired to herd the horses in and after they found out I was a ball player they kept me. Charles Martine, Old Man Martine's stepson was there too. He was half-brother to George. They had the same mother but different fathers.[84] We all played on this team. Duffy was short-stop.

They were going to have a fair at Newkirk. Our team went over there. The Newkirk manager talked to McGowan and wanted Martine and me to play at the fair. He was willing to give us seven dollars a game and all expenses and board. Mr. McGowan said all right. They sent a hack for us in the evening, and we took the equipment and went down. They put us up in a hotel. In the afternoon we played in a game. They had a Kaw Indian named Bluejacket on our team.[85] Charlie Martine pitched for us. We won the first game and lost the next. Then they took us back to Chilocco again.

Now they were organizing another league team. Boys were trying out every day. They didn't put Charlie Martine on. Duffy and I were put on,[86] and Sam Morris was on too. This was a Chilocco team. We played in Oklahoma City for the first game. Sam Morris was a good pitcher, and we won the game. Then the Oklahoma City team came to Chilocco. We won again. They wouldn't play us any more.

We were practicing hard. The team was supported by the government.[87] A few of the players were paid. I was getting fifty dollars, Morris was getting a hundred and twenty-five, Teeboo, one hundred, John Rood, a pitcher, was getting a hundred. Duffy didn't get anything. He was a student at the school, so they didn't pay him. There was a part-Mexican, part-Pueblo boy named Rudy Santefugas on the team. He was a Chilocco student too.[88] There were about three students on the team. All the rest were ex-students. We all stayed right at the school, lived there. Most of those on the team were men who had played ball for them in 1895 when I was just a kid at the school and couldn't play at all.[89] Now I could play right along with them and maybe better than they. Duffy played short-stop or third and changed with me. One game I would play one and he would play the other, the next day we'd change places. We played some good league teams in Oklahoma. Then one of our best players turned pro and the team broke up. It was this way.

We went to Joplin, Missouri and played the Joplin league team. Joplin paid all expenses. A big fair was going on, and they were charging admission to the games. They beat us the first game 3 to 2. The next day we played them in an eleven-inning game and won, 1 to 0. Morris pitched. They offered him a hundred and fifty dollars to join their team right there, and he took it, and that broke up our team. He stayed with them and pitched for them for seven years. Joe Teeboo went back to the coast.

2. Sam Chino on horseback. Date and photographer unknown. Courtesy of the Smithsonian Institution National Museum of the American Indian, Photography Collection, #N53211.

It was 1902 now. Vacation time came. The Chilocco children were all going home. Charlie Martine and I got on a salaried team. We signed up for sixty dollars a month and board, They came after us from Ponca City. Bluejacket was on that team too.[90] A fellow by the name of James Baldwin was managing the team. We played for two months.

Then Charlie Martine got a job at the Indian school as disciplinarian. So I quit too. I went to Tonkawa and played with the Tonkawa team.[91] I stayed in town. They paid my board and five dollars a game. I stayed about a month and then got tired of them. That was my second time in Tonkawa. In 1898 I had come through there just to size up the place. That was when I was coming back to Fort Sill from school.

After I quit the Tonkawa team I went to Fort Sill. There I found Duffy on the team, and they had a crack nine there. I played with

3. Sam Kenoi and Laurence Mithlo. Date and photographer unknown. Eve Ball Papers, MSS 3096, series 4, box 58, folder 42. L. Tom Perry Collection, Harold B. Lee Library, Courtesy of Brigham Young University.

that team all summer. I worked here and there besides. I had come back too late to do farming of my own.

About the middle of October I made up my mind to go back to Chilocco. I went back with a lot of children. They asked me what grade I was in. I said third grade. Every week I went up; they'd make me go into a higher grade. "You are fooling us, Sam," they said. They put me in the seventh, eighth, then the ninth grade. Still I belonged higher. They wouldn't let me go to school. Their school only went to ninth grade.

So the superintendent called me in. He said, "Sam, you're beyond our ninth grade. You can stay here, and we'll give you a job as assistant to the boy's disciplinarian."

Charlie Martine was disciplinarian. He had come from his job at the Ute Indian School. He was the adjutant. I was adjutant too. He had charge of the big boys and girls I had charge of the younger ones.[92] We were drilling the children and putting them through athletics. They told me that I had gone as high as I could there, and that I could go home if I wanted to, or I could stay. They let me stay because I was a good athlete and was playing baseball and football for them. They told me I could stay on the agreement that I would obey all the rules and work at some trade. So I stayed and we each had a battalion and had to drill the students every day.

I went into the wagon shop. It didn't take me long to learn to make wagons, and good ones too. Towards spring I worked in the bakery shop. Then in spring, close to vacation, I was on the ball team and the relay team, too. And I ran the mile race and the two-mile race. Duffy was the leading man in pole vault. There were all kinds of Indians there, but Duffy was best at pole vault. He went into big contests and won. They didn't pay Duffy and me for the baseball we played then. Duffy was a student at school, and I agreed to work for them just for my keep.

2

Dan Nicholas's School Years, as told by Himself

Dan Nicholas was born at Fort Sill, Indian Territory, on March 30, 1894 (Delgadillo 2013, 208). His father was James Nicholas, "a famous Chiricahua runner" (Ball 197?),[1] and his mother was Elsie Nicholas. James Nicholas, as shown in figure 1 in the introduction, was also a bugler for Apache scout Company I (Skinner 1987, 355), and "his tribe's first professional musician" (375–76). His son Dan attended the mission school of the Fort Sill Dutch Reformed Church both as a day student and as a boarder, and he says a great deal about his experiences there. His mother having died when he was about eight, Dan Nicholas lived with his grandmother when not at school. After her death two years later, he went to live with an aunt named Bessie Hunlona, his mother's half-sister (Delgadillo 2013, 115). Consistent with Apache matrilineal practice, he did not live with his father, but he makes clear that the two were on good terms. He says that his father sometimes visited him while he was boarding at the Fort Sill mission school, and also that he occasionally stayed at his father's home.

Dan Nicholas attended the Chilocco Indian School from 1907 to 1911, but he says almost nothing about his time there, like Sam Kenoi omitting the usual *topoi* and *loci* of boarding school life. He may have come back to Fort Sill for the summers—Fort Sill is a little over two hundred miles south of Chilocco—but again, whether he did or not, or what his reasons were for doing so or not are not matters he takes up. Not long after leaving Chilocco, he was sent to the Haskell Institute—as a punishment, as he explains—from which he soon ran away;

on being returned to the school, he did not stay long. Like Chilocco, Haskell was one of the more important of the federal Indian boarding schools, but it seems to have had little interest for Dan Nicholas, and he once more tells us nothing about his time there, again and again returning to memories of the mission school and representing his experiences in some detail.

Nicholas, unlike Sam Kenoi, generally admired Geronimo, who allowed him and some of his youthful contemporaries to attend healing ceremonies he performed at Fort Sill. We have seen that Kenoi, to a degree unusual for an Apache, did not at all fear ghosts, but Nicholas's ghost-fright was very strong, as he describes fully. He worked not only with Morris Opler but, like Kenoi, with the anthropologist Harry Hoijer, and in 1939 published a piece of ethnographic work of his own, a brief essay on the "Mescalero Apache Girl's Puberty Ceremony." Many years later, in 1960 and 1963, he was consultant to the amateur ethnologist and linguist Guy Tyler, who elicited from him a number of Mescalero Apache words that he captured on a reel-to-reel tape recorder (Tyler 1960, 1963). Eve Ball interviewed Nicholas several times between 1966 and 1968, and in a note to James Kaywaykla's autobiography, *In the Days of Victorio*, she writes that both he and Sam Kenoi had "died before 1970" (Kaywaykla 1970, xv).

Fort Sill Apache tribal historian Michael Darrow informed me that Nicholas "received an allotment of land in Oklahoma and was considered to be a member of the Fort Sill Apache Tribe," although he "moved to Mescalero soon after allotment and remained there." He says as well that he "had a daughter Rowena and had two granddaughters, one of whom was still living" in 2021, and also that a granddaughter of Nicholas's younger sister, Minnie Nicholas Zurega, was alive and living at Mescalero (Darrow, pers. comm., July 28, 2021). I have been unsuccessful in contacting any of them.

For one reason or another, all proper names were underlined in Morris Opler's typescript of Dan Nicholas's autobiography, and I have removed the underlining. Punctuation is sparse and I have added nothing to what Opler wrote. There are a few lengthy paragraphs, but the typescript for the most part uses shorter ones that break more often than one might expect. As was occasionally the case with Sam Kenoi's autobiographical narrative, this may represent something about Nicholas's manner of narration—or something in any text he composed himself—or it may have been Opler's choice, perhaps to suggest pauses in an oral narrative. In any case, I have again made no changes to the paragraphing of the original. As with the Kenoi typescript, I have silently corrected typos or very minor errors, and I have indicated some very few ellipses with three dots.

Although Nicholas's words—like Kenoi's—were probably edited substantially, at several points in the typescript there remain what I find odd shifts of subject, with no transitions, and throughout the narrative the chronology differs from what one might expect in a conventional Western life history. It would not be accurate to call the ordering of events "circular," but it is definitely not "linear," and I suspect this very likely represents Nicholas's actual manner of narration (or composition), and that Opler did not substantially rearrange the materials as they were presented. Following are pp. 41–100 of the Dan Nicholas autobiography as contained in the Morris Opler Papers at Cornell University's Karl A Kroch Library, box 35, folder 15, and box 36, folder 1.

> Very often when Naiche was going off in his horse and buggy we would climb up behind when he wasn't looking and steal a ride.[2] Once I got caught in the spokes of the wheel in this way. I got spun around two or three times. I was afraid to holler. I got out of it some way. But I nearly got my leg broken. Boys and girls played together at this time.[3]
>
> When I was about eight years old my mother died.[4] She wasn't sick long. She died right in the house. I have a faint recollection of her being sick in the house. I didn't go to the funeral. They don't let young people of my age go to funerals. My grandmother took care of the body.
>
> While my mother was very sick my sister and I stayed over at our grandmother's. After my mother died we continued staying right there. While at my grandmother's I went to school during the day. Minnie was not going to school yet.[5]

The school was about four miles from my grandmother's. We children had a bus to pick us up and take us.[6] The agent decided that I was to go to school. He sent a notice to my grandmother. I wanted to go anyway. We didn't have to take any lunch. The government served all the children a good meal at noon. All the grades were in one room, but they sat in different parts of the room. One teacher taught all the subjects to the groups. She was a woman teacher. The school was a mission school, but the government took care of all the financial part of it, like the dinner, etc. I don't know who paid the teachers, perhaps the government, maybe some board of the church. It was the Dutch Reformed Church.[7] They had some children there whom they called orphans, who stayed there all the time. The first two years I came home to my grandmother's at night. After my second year they took off the bus and all the children had to walk. I used to walk about half-way, mostly, and then go in swimming. (But I used to slip off the bus about half the time before that too.) The truant officer was always chasing us. We were reported to the superintendent. She used to punish us and report us to our folks. My grandmother used to scold me, but I disliked a scolding more than a whipping. When we walked we used to catch up with certain boys and bunches we knew, and have a good time. It was lots of fun.

My grandmother used to buy me new shoes. She'd say, "Now keep those shoes on," and I'd promise to. But it is warm in Oklahoma in spring and summer and we boys liked to go barefooted; so just as soon as I was out of sight of the house off would come the shoes. I'd hide them some place and pick them up on the way back. Sometimes I'd forget where I had put them.

The government used to issue shoes at school too. They took it for granted that you had no shoes if you showed up without any. I was afraid to admit that I had left the shoes on some creek-bank, and so it happened that I sometimes had six pairs of shoes in the woods somewhere. I had all the shoes *I* wanted. Very often I would put my books in some sheltered place and go off playing all day with the boys in the mountains. Then at night we'd gather up our books under our arms and come walking in as though we had been at school all day. "What did you learn today?" my grandmother would ask. "Oh, I learned a lot, I'll soon be able to talk good English," I'd say, and throw down my cap as though I were tired and ask for something to eat.

The children in the school ranged from four to nineteen years in age. The youngest were not in classes, but were living there because they were orphans. Some were mere babies. But there were children from six to nineteen in the classes.

The superintendent was a woman, a missionary. All the teachers were missionaries. There was only one man, a white boy who was taking care of the mission farm.

We had a preacher who came to the school to preach every Sunday. He was from the Comanche mission church.[8]

We got to school a little before nine. The bell rang three times and we went right in. There was only one teacher for all classes above kindergarten. There was a kindergarten teacher too. I went to kindergarten first. Was there six months. A nice old lady was teacher. She taught me English. Then I got into the regular classes.

We would always have a reading from the Bible first. Then we went on with class work. At ten we had a twenty minute recess. We played games then—marbles, kites, ball—everything. Then went back and worked till noon. Then we marched over to the mess building and had a good meal.

Every day the teacher selected one boy and one girl to go over and help the cook. They had to peel potatoes, chop wood, etc. At first I hated this. If I thought it was near my turn I'd skip school or come in late on purpose. I'd wait till I saw someone go over to do the work and then I came in as though I had been late. A few years later, when I was more grown up, I liked to go though. Whenever a pretty girl was chosen I'd volunteer. I liked washing dishes pretty well then. Before that I was ashamed of it. It was woman's work.

After lunch we had recess for a while, and then went back at one. School lasted till four. We had recess again at about two-thirty.

At lunch grace was said too. On Sunday, the children who stayed at the mission boarding school had to go to church. We who came from home did not have to go. It was up to our folks. My grandmother did not make me go.

There were about six or seven grades in the school. Sometimes I got a little behind in my work because of so much fooling around. But by the end of the year I was pretty well caught up. I was always the smallest in my class. I know that the teacher thought I was getting along well.

One of the reasons I stayed out a lot was because they went over the things so much. I'd know what was coming and that's why I wouldn't care if I went or not. Some of the Indian children are pretty dumb at schoolwork, you know.

The teacher used to take a switch to the boys if they did something. She made the girls do extra work. We would get whipped for talking back, for throwing paper wads or erasers at the girls, etc. Some of the bigger boys used to resist the teacher when she tried to hit them. I used to think this was great, for I was so scared I used to bend for mine. The teacher would tap you on the hand with the ruler. I used to get punished about twice a week. She would also make us stay in or stand in a corner.

One time a whole bunch of us were involved in stealing and eating some candy left over from Christmas. We were tied, each by the wrist, in a long row, and made to go to dinner that way. One boy, who was a kind of a cry-baby, began to yell as though he were stabbed when they started to tie him up. Then when we were to go to dinner, he balked—he sat down and wouldn't budge. We finally had to drag him along. I sure had to laugh.

During these first years at school I went around with Nelson, Robert Goody, John Tonitu, and others from the village.[9]

John Allard and I met there about this time. He had just come from Mexico with his mother. I just knew him slightly. He was from the other village.[10]

School would start in September, and would be out in the early part of May.

Christmas was the big event. We would have a big party then.

Sometimes mothers and fathers came to school to see their children. Naiche used to come. Then the teacher would ask him to talk to us in Indian.[11]

At schools we had plays, and singing, and speaking for entertainment. I never took part in plays, but I did have to recite speeches and poems. John Allard used to sing. They say he had a good voice when he was young. I had to recite things, like Lincoln's "Gettysburg Address." The teacher used to train me. I had to make certain gestures. I guess John Allard was a good singer. At least his voice used to go way high. I used to tease him about it; I used to call him a girl. Some of the other boys used to tease him too. He wore a big wide blouse and a bow tie. He looked like a sissy to me.

Often on the way to school we used to gather wild grapes. We passed farms and used to take melons too. The farmers (Indians) saw us and would chase us.

It sure was a beautiful place. There were so many creeks. I believe any boy would have done as I did about skipping school. In spring it was sure beautiful, and the birds were singing. At the place where we used to go swimming (at Loco's village)[12] there was a cliff of overhanging white rock. Every Saturday afternoon the boys from both villages used to meet here and swim. We dammed the creek up for swimming and fishing.

Once at Four Mile Crossing we found a bee hive in the ground.[13] They are pretty mean over there, we teased them so. I was told to put my foot on the hive and to let out only one bee at a time. As it came out the other boys would kill it. We all had netting on our heads and hands. But there were so many of them that I got tired and let too many out at once. They came out and stung me and then I ran off—letting them all out. We surely were stung. I had a bump on the back of my head (I was shaved); one boy had a double chin; another had a big bump on the nose. We had not noticed, but a lot of whites had come along the road and were watching. They were having a good time out of it.

We used to push the boys who rode a bicycle to school into the creek. We'd say, "Let me give you a start," and then push them into the creek.

On Sundays, instead of going to church, most of the Indians would gather at Four Mile Crossing where they would have baseball (Indian), gambling, pole and hoop games, horse races, or rock game.[14] One week there would be just horse races. Next time foot races. Girls never took part in these. The Comanches would come in and take part. Some white people came in and raced for a while. But someone kicked about it and then only the Indians did it. Some men would go out on a coyote hunt too. This kept up for a number of years; went on for a few years after I stayed at boarding school. First it was at Four Mile Crossing. Then it went on at Geronimo's village. The mission and government must have opposed it, for from this time on, it began to die out. All the people used to start to the place early in the morning.

At school I was kind of scared of the teacher when I did wrong, but when I was good I wasn't afraid of her.

We celebrated Easter and Valentine's day too. We made valentines in school. When we took them home the old people couldn't understand what they were for. They laughed at us.

During this time my father was living in his old home. I didn't see him so much. He was paying for my support though. I'd see him at Old Man Katizini's when I went over there.[15]

In the evening we would eat and then play till about eight or nine; then we went to bed.

I was about eight or nine now. It was about this time that I learned that Sam Bindi was a witch.[16] My grandmother told me so. Also I heard the other children say it. One time he came to Naiche's village. We children were playing around there. We ducked around the houses because they said he was a witch. I heard one man talking and saying that Bindi had tried to get married a number of time, but he was always refused because he was a witch.[17] They told us to keep out of his sight as much as possible, to refuse any gift from him, and not to let him do anything queer to us. Also to treat him with respect when we met him so he wouldn't do anything harmful to us. We were told not to offend him under any circumstances.

About this time I guess my father thought I was getting too wild and staying out of school too much. Perhaps my grandmother complained to my father. Anyway he told the agent that my grandmother was too old to take care of me, and that he thought I would get better care if I stayed at the mission school. John Tonitu's mother decided to send him there at the same time. So we went together. I was about ten years old at this time.

Under this arrangement I stayed all during the week at school and came to my grandmother's Saturday morning. I had to be back to school Saturday evening. After a short while my grandmother died and I stayed Saturdays at Bessie's.

Bessie had three boys about four to six years old. I had to take care of the darn little suckers.[18] I haven't forgiven those boys for that yet. I was ashamed of it. I was like a nurse to them. John Tonitu was there too. He used to run off from this job most of the time. I used to drag the oldest kid around in one of those little red wagons. I used to take it into a rough place and knock him off. I used to give those boys a good kick.

Bessie was in Geronimo's village. John Allard lived in this village. His mother was pretty strict with him. He used to say he envied us when we went by. But he managed to get out with us sometimes.

When school let out for the summer I stayed at Bessie's. We used to go over and see Geronimo and get him to tell us stories. The boys I went around with at this time were John Allard, John Tonitu, Clarence (who stayed with Mrs. Stevens), Grover Kaitah, and Paul Gedelkin, Jr.[19]

Geronimo used to let us in when he was curing. Most medicine men do not allow young boys in.

Geronimo used to tell us coyote stories.[20] He was a very funny fellow. Had no sense of humor. Everything he says strikes the other people as funny. His choice of words was funny. He didn't mean to be funny, but he took everything so serious that lots of people had a lot of fun with him. He was very absent minded too. He would be looking for his hat and he would have it on his head. One time when we were over to visit him he was making a bow with a big knife. Pretty soon he began asking his wife where his knife was. All the while he had it in his hand, but we didn't let on. So there he was, scolding his wife and telling her to look for it for him. He was built like Fatty and wasn't active any more.[21] That's why he wanted his wife to get it for him. But she wouldn't look. She said, "You're old enough to look after your own knife." Geronimo got pretty mad. "Boys, you see how she is," he said. "I advise you not to get married." Finally he saw the knife in his hand. "Why, I'm nothing but a damn fool," he said.

Because he took everything so seriously they were always playing jokes on him. Once Old Man Katizini told Geronimo that Charlie Icti was his enemy and was going to shoot him on sight.[22] Geronimo took it seriously. He said, "Why, I treated that fellow better than anyone else, and then he goes around talking about me like that." No one told him the truth. Sometimes Indians joke in this way. The next day Geronimo cut himself a big cane and carried it around with him. A few days later he and Charlie came face to face in the street in Lawton. Charlie stopped to talk to Geronimo, but Geronimo kept going. Then Icti said, "Hey, what are you carrying that big stick for? Don't you know that a lot of white people don't like you and might take that stick away and club you with it?" Geronimo answered, "Yes, and I hear that there are a lot of Indians who don't like me and who want to do me harm." Charlie saw that there was something wrong and demanded to know what it was. Then Geronimo told him right out that he knew that Icti had threatened to shoot him at sight. He said, "And that's why I made this big stick for you." Charlie clapped his hand to his mouth in amazement. Then he tried to convince Geronimo that he had never said such a thing. Finally he invited Geronimo to have a beer with him at a saloon but Geronimo didn't want to go. He thought it was a trap, that Charlie wanted to get him drunk and do him harm. It took Icti a long time to convince him.

Geronimo was not required to work.[23] Instead he spent all his time making bows. He could write his name and did it with real Indian paint.[24]

Geronimo didn't show much emotion. He used to keep his face straight no matter how he felt, just laughing when he wanted to. Naiche was a lot different.

Geronimo had ghost power and coyote power.[25] He had other ceremonies too. When we came to his ceremonies he would warn us not to scratch ourselves with our nails or we would get a shocking sensation right then and there. Geronimo was a Ndendai. He got his power from Asa's father. Some say he was related to Asa's father. I think he was. Asa says that Geronimo is related to him.[26] Geronimo asked Asa's father to give him his ceremonies, and his own prominence came from his association with Asa's father.

Once Geronimo wanted to say something to the agent.[27] He thought that people had not been interpreting correctly for him. So he took Arnold Kinzuni and asked him to interpret for him.[28] "Now you're just a mouthpiece," he told Kinzuni. "You say exactly what I tell you. People haven't been saying what I tell them, and I want you to remember that you are not saying this, you're just acting for me and should say just what I tell you." "All right, I speak good English," said Kinzuni, "go ahead and speak." So Geronimo stated his case. At the end the agent asked, "What did he say?" "He says you are a damn fool," was what Kinzuni told him. Of course Geronimo had not said this at all. The agent just laughed and walked away. Later we told Geronimo what Arnold had done. Geronimo took a stick and went out to find Kinzuni. When he saw him he tried to hit him with the stick.

About this time Geronimo was working on a history of his life. Esa acted as interpreter. Mr. Bartlett, who took it down, was connected with the school system of Lawton.[29]

We have people who always like to be around when anyone is sick. As soon as they hear about it they go over, even before the family knows. And they always offer advice and tell what medicine man to have, etc. Mrs. Uncas is like that. She always tried to get a lot of information about me too. She is always asking my wife about me. If I am away from camp for a few days she will come around and say, "Where's that man?" My wife knows that she is just hunting for gossip and says, "Why, what's the matter with you, you always seem to be pretty interested in that man." She knows Mrs. Uncas is that way and is always kidding her. Mrs. Uncas will say, "Oh, I thought he had left you." Then my wife says, "No, he's only over to the sheep range for a few days." Such people like to be right there when a curing is taking place.

When you are sick, if you are well known and liked, many people will come and visit you, out of respect though. These are not busybodies.

The first ceremony I saw of Geronimo's was one for an older man. Some coyote or dog had made him sick.[30] We heard that the ceremony was going to be held through one boy who had got hold of the news. It was held at Geronimo's place. We asked him if we could attend. He said it would be all right, but told us not to make any noise or to scratch ourselves, that's all. It began in the evening, as soon as it was dark. Geronimo had a *tsa* before him filled with the things used for the ceremony. It was an old black basket. He had a feather (eagle-downy) in there, and a shell (*ditcile*), and a bag of *tadidin*.[31] It is all I remember that was in the basket. I think he smoked to the directions first of all, beginning with the east. He used Bull Durham and rolled his own cigarette. He just puffed once to each direction. Then he threw the cigarette away. Then he started to sing. The songs are about coyote. There were lots of songs. They told how coyote helped Geronimo. They said that coyote was a slick fellow, that he was hard to see and find, that he gave these characteristics to Geronimo so that he could make himself invisible and even turn into a door. The songs were all on this order. The singing went on till about midnight. The patient lay stretched out before Geronimo. The ceremony did not take place in Geronimo's house but in the arbor outside. There was a fire there. Geronimo and the patient were on the west side of the fire. Before the singing and after the smoking Geronimo rubbed the patient with *tadidin*. He dropped the pollen on the patient, just on certain parts of the body. He prayed to the directions as he did this. These prayers referred to coyote and were on the same order as the songs which followed. He used the curved stick for the drum when he began singing.

At midnight he stopped singing and all went home. Geronimo stopped singing when the evening star (*sostso*) was half way between the horizon and straight up in the sky. This is the Indian midnight. Some Indians went by the big dipper, the seven stars. This group starts in the east at night and is in the west in the morning. When it got to the position of the sun at noon, the ceremonial man would stop singing.

Some older people were there. They were mostly relatives of the sick man. But it would be all right for anyone to come in and watch. We sat in circular fashion in the back of the shelter. But the space to the east was left open, as always happened at a ceremony. This was a four day ceremony. The same songs, prayers and procedure was gone through for the four days.[32] At the end of each song Geronimo gave a call like a coyote.

This was the only ceremony that I ever saw Geronimo give. I know that he had ghost power too. That night he told some of the boys that he was going to give another ceremony for a patient on another night, this time for ghost sickness, and that they might attend if they could promise not to scratch themselves.

Geronimo had a garden. Every now and then he'd take a watermelon out, cut it up under his arbor and say, "Come on boys." He liked watermelon pretty well himself.

He used to tell us, "Don't smoke until you have caught a coyote on foot boys. That's an old Apache custom."

There were many ceremonies going on at this time but we boys did not attend them. It was too common for us to bother about. We were familiar with the customs of our people and didn't pay much attention to it. It was pretty hard for us younger people to attend. There were always restrictions on whoever was there. For some ceremonies you couldn't scratch, for some you couldn't leave before it was all over, for some you couldn't sleep. So we didn't care much about being there. But we always went to the tepee ceremony, for you could always have a good time there.[33]

When September came around I stayed at the mission school entirely. The only time I got away was Saturday. Bessie would call for John and me, and bring us back in the evening. We had to be back for supper.

At the mission school we had a dormitory. The boys slept in one end, the girls in the other. The age range was from about six to fourteen. We had all sorts of little duties. We had to get up and make fires when detailed, or we had to chop wood. On Saturdays we had to chop a lot of wood so that no work would be done on Sunday. Two were detailed to take care of the beds and sweep out on the boys' side. Two had to help in the laundry. One used to build fires in the little children's dormitory (which was in another building), so that it would be warm for the children when they woke up. This was my job mostly.

There was a young woman over there taking care of those children. I had to make a fire for her too. She used to get up naked before me and start dressing. I was about fourteen years old then. So I didn't mind that job, but volunteered for it all the time. Now that I think back on it I believe that she tried to tempt me. She was a young woman, there were no white men around there, and she was probably sex starved. But at that time I didn't take advantage of it. I was pretty young, and besides my Indian training helped me. For I was trained at Indian camps where it is hard to be private and where we were trained to pay no attention to such a thing.

But I did tell John Allard about it. I told him that he could come along with me the next morning if he would be a good actor and make believe he was just coming to help me. John is a good actor, and so the next morning he came with me and started carrying in a big load of wood, just as though he was coming to help make the fire. When we both walked in she took one look at John and said, "John Allard, get out of here." She was in bed and didn't get out till he was gone. I paid no attention but just made believe that I was going on with my work. I sure laughed at John. When I saw John later that day he was pretty excited. He said he wanted that job. I think he would have done something about it. But I didn't have any intentions of asking her anything. I was afraid to. I always used to make believe I didn't see anything.

Once a bunch of us got into the girls' dormitory. Every Wednesday evening there was a prayer meeting. All of us didn't have to go, and once a bunch of us who had stayed home got into the girls' dormitory. We didn't do much but showed them ours, and they showed us theirs. It was just a trip to the museum. It was never found out. Allard, John Tonitu and I were in on it.

Another thing the boys did was to bore a little hole in the wall of the girls' dormitory and talk to the girls through it.

The first money I ever earned was gotten from making a fire in the morning for the white boy who tended the mission farm. I did this in a hurry, before I went on detail. I got fifty cents a month for this. He used me as a butler and stayed in bed till it was nice and warm.

I was pretty slim when I was a kid. They used to make me eat a raw egg every evening. I used to be pretty afraid too. I was influenced a great deal by the Indian beliefs about ghosts, and used to get scared as soon as the lights went out at night.[34] I'd go over to someone else's bed and force myself on them. I'd do this to John Allard, for instance, though we had single beds. Often I'd wake up screaming in the middle of the night thinking that I had seen someone with a white sheet on near my bed. The matron would have to come in and stroke my head and hold my hand. I'd dream of ghosts. A face would be bending over me laughing. It would just be an outline, no features showing. Sometimes it would be dark, sometimes white. I would not dream about actual events or people.

When I was about fourteen years old I got in trouble over a girl.[35] Some bigger boys, about sixteen years old, were going after a certain Comanche girl, who was pretty and whom they liked, and were going to hold her down and force her. I didn't understand clearly just what it was all about, but it sounded pretty exciting and so I tagged along. They tried to overpower the girl but she struggled and got away. She went right back to the school and told on us. The other boys put all the blame on me and I didn't get a chance to explain. As a result I got a good strapping.

There was no masturbation among the Apache boys at the school. It is against the Apache nature to handle the private organ. There was one boy there, a Comanche, who did it and who advised John Allard and myself to do it. We thought it was a shameful thing to do. I can hardly believe that it is so common among the whites. What Martine told you about the old time Apaches is true.[36] It was not done. We children were never warned against it. It was never mentioned, thought of, or considered. We got no instruction about sex at all in this way.

While staying at the mission school we could no longer get to the Indian games on Sunday. On Sundays we were not allowed off the mission grounds. We had to go to Sunday school and church. No games were allowed either. The place was run on a basis of old time religion.

At nine we had to be in bed. Before the lamps were blown out the matron would come in and lead us in prayer. Each one knelt by his bed and said a prayer. "Now I lay me down to sleep." We just took it as a matter of course. There was no resentment because we had to pray so much.

On Sunday morning we all went into the school building at about nine. We sang religious songs and then divided into Sunday school classes.

We used an International Sunday School text book.[37] I have seen it since. It was about characters in the Bible and events of the Bible. There was no cutting up in Sunday school. They were very strict. Class lasted about a half hour to an hour. Then we all went back to church, where the regular service was being held for outsiders as well as the children. Old Man Cooney, James Koakly (who also interpreted sometimes), Sam Haozous and Jason Betzini, who married one of the missionaries at the school. They were all prominent members of the church. Also Carlos Kinny, an Apache boy who married one of the missionaries named Pierce.[38] These marriages occurred when the mission school broke up, when the Chiricahuas were moving out. But those families stayed behind. Mrs. Kinny lost her husband and is now living in Alamogordo. I saw their girl, who is about thirteen years old, not long ago. She is a very beautiful child and looks a bit Indian.[39] Mrs. Kinny is now married again.

At the school we had regular examinations. Had a midyear and final. I went through all the grades. They didn't have any formal graduation. You were just through when you finished up the grades.

There was no chance to play hookey at the school. Had to attend every day.

There was a creek about a half mile away from the school. We weren't supposed to go swimming, but we did. We often saved white people from drowning. Once three soldiers came in swimming. Two could swim and one could not. The first two tried to get the other fellow to come in. But for a long while he only paddled around the bank. Finally, when the others were far out, he decided to come in. He went in a deep spot and began to go down. The others hollered to us to save him. So we got under him and got him out. It was a hard job too for he was struggling like wild. He was angry when he got out; he got dressed and left the other two.

This was a tremendous place to swim. The fellow for whom I built a fire in the morning got drowned here. He went out swimming with a theological student who was staying at the school for a time. About four o'clock in the afternoon the student came back all excited, saying that the boy had drowned. He said that he was quite a distance from the fellow when he started to go down. We went to find the body. Dove to locate it. When we found it, Eugene Chihuahua took it out.[40]

The student said that he must have got cramps for he went right down. He said that he had not suffered, that God had taken him, and things like this. The other missionaries all talked that way too. They spoke at table of what a good boy he had been, how he had always gone to church, and I could tell from their remarks they thought that God had just chosen this way to take him without any suffering. But this sounded very stupid to me. From what I know of swimming I thought that he could have been saved. I believed that the student was afraid to get near and help him, because a drowning person struggles so.

John Tuisga was a boy a couple of years older than I, and a lot bigger, who was staying at the school.[41] His mother was dead too. He was a great hand for fishing; he always had a pole in his hand. Others would try all day and then he would come along in the same spot and catch a string of fish.

Once I went along with him because I wanted to and helped him. Later we had a fight over a marble game and he found out he could lick me. After that when he saw me alone he would make me go fishing with him. He even made me dig the worms for him. He told me that he would make me sorry if I told the matron, so I was afraid to do that. He'd make me come along and hold the fish he caught in the water to keep them fresh. He would not even let me cough. I had to sit there for hours and hours. Every once in a while he would throw up his line and I'd have to put on a worm and throw it back. I began to drop pebbles into the water when he wasn't looking, hoping that the fish would be scared away, and that he'd get discouraged and go home. But it only made him worse. He sure could stay on. So I found by experience that dropping the pebbles didn't work. Once he caught me dropping the pebbles in. He began to call me down. "What the hell are you doing," he yelled.

When we were in a crowd I used to get even with him by teasing him. I'd say, "Hello there, fisherman." He sure would get pretty mad.

Once he took me to his favorite fishing place. There was a log extending into the water. He made me sit on the outside where I couldn't run away. I had to sit there about three hours. He wouldn't let me cough or spit. He just sat there like a kingfisher, so still. It was getting on my nerves. Finally he brought his line up and told me to bait it. I said I would but that I was tired and wanted to go to the bank for a minute. He was sitting on the log, too, with his feet dangling over one side of it. I told him I'd bait his hook if he'd let me step over him and go to the bank. "All right, hurry up," he said. So I walked over his lap and just as I passed I took hold of his head and gave him a good push. He went backwards, his feet in the air, and I just kept going. I took his string of fish and threw them at him. "There's your old fish," I said and I made for the mission. I could hear him swearing at me as he went down.

It took him about twenty minutes to get out and then he came after me. I saw him coming but kept the same distance between us. He didn't gain on me at all. I went right in to where the matron was. "Good afternoon, Mrs. ______," I said, and began talking to her. "Why, what makes you so nice today, Dan?" she asked. By this time John had come up and was waiting for me. But I followed the matron all over. Finally I asked her if she would read to me in her room, but she said she had no time. She didn't know what it was all about. "No, go out and play," she said. "I can't. John here is just waiting to beat me up. He made me stay with him all the morning while he was fishing," I said. "No, he's just making it up," John told her. She just passed it off. But it was important to me with him hanging around. So I hung around her all the afternoon and John didn't get a chance at me. He seemed to forget it after that, but he never bothered me to go with him again. I guess I cured him. After this I got in with older boys and didn't let him catch me alone. Before that he had got me into a lot of trouble. He would keep me out long after meal times and then blame it on me when we got back, saying that I asked him to stay longer, or asked him to go with me. I never had a chance to explain. They looked on him as an older boy and more reliable.

He used to bring his fish back and have them cooked as an extra for him and his table mates. If I were at his table I'd get some, but if I were not, I didn't get any, even if I had been out helping him.[42] I have never liked to fish since.

My grandmother died during my first year at school. Old Man Tonitu was going by and told me.[43] I didn't go home at the time. I didn't take it very hard. I didn't understand it very well.

Once in the schoolroom I got into a fight with Vincent Bindi.[44] It was during recess. We were playing ball. I wanted to be pitcher. He didn't like that. But I put myself in as pitcher anyway. So he went on the other side. When he came up to bat I hit him in the head just for meanness. He got mad and started to walk towards me. He started to fight. By the time the bell rang we each had a black eye. When we came in the teacher saw that we had been fighting and called us up in the front of the room. She asked what it was about and I told her that while we were playing I had hit him accidentally with a ball, and he had started to walk towards me and fight. Then she tried to get me to kiss him. I wouldn't do it. She was trying to make me. She tried to grab me by the hair and force me to him, but my hair was shaved off and I always slipped away. It was so funny I started to laugh. We were up on a little platform in the front of the room. Finally, after being pushed around all I could stand, I said, "All right, I'll kiss him," and I hit him in the other eye, knocking him off the platform. Everyone was surprised and started to laugh. The teacher began to hit me with the ruler she had in her hand.

But Vincent became my good friend after that. He was mad for a few days and then seemed to go out of his way to be my friend. He gave me chewing tobacco, and smokes. He asked me to go fishing with him.

I had had a taste of chewing tobacco before this. John Allard and I had gone with Watson Mailo to the creek.[45] We were lying under the trees. Watson was an older boy and was chewing. He asked us if we wanted a chew. We said, "Yes," and asked how to chew it. He told us to chew a lot till you got a mouthful of juice and then to swallow the juice. It sure made us sick for the whole day. Watson laughed and laughed.

At home I had smoked leaves once in a while, and rarely got hold of a cigarette, but here at school about this time I really began to smoke. Some of the boys kept the tobacco out in the woodshed. We rolled our own. The missionaries didn't know it. We didn't smoke around the buildings.

There was one girl who was always telling on me. We had been good friends, but I teased her so much that she got to hate me. I used to like to see her get mad. I used to bring a thin piece of wood into class. It would bend and I would put a spit ball on it and aim at her. I also brought in the Apache popgun and shot at her with it. She always used to tell on me, so I started to call her "tattle-tale." Everyone got to calling her that. I used to say "by golly" in front of her and she'd start right off like a car in high to tell on me. I'd get scolded for saying that or "gracious Lord." It used to be worth it to see her marching off to tell on me. Later I wanted to be friends with her, but she wouldn't talk to me.

Some of the children used to make little tepees, covered with grass and just high enough for two to get under. They called this playing "husband and wife." They used to make mud pies, take them in and play night had come. (Goodness knows what took place in there.) (laughter).[46] I used to say I'd take this girl for my wife, and it sure would get her mad. I didn't play this though. I was one of those who knocked down the tepees on them and stepped on the mud pies.

I got into a fight with Watson Mailo too. We were playing football. He claimed I hit him and gave me a good licking. After that we were on the outs. I called him "the fox" because of his name, and all the boys took it up.[47]

Christmas morning Don Tuisga, brother of John came down the steps crying as if he had been stabbed.[48] He was always crying. We called him "the Baby." Sometimes he would cry for almost nothing. If you said "Good morning" to him, he would cry. This time I asked him what the matter was and he told me that Hugh Coonie had taken his candy away from him. "Well, where is that sucker?" I asked. "He's over making a fire in the laundry," the kid said.[49] "Well, come along, I'll get your candy pretty fast," I said. But he didn't want to go. So I went over to the laundry. Hugh was making a fire, bending over the stove, throwing matches in. "What's Don crying for?" I asked him. "What business is it of yours?" he said. "Well, you'd better give him his candy back," I told him. "Get out of here," he said and kicked me. Then I hit him in the side of the face and we began fighting. While we were fighting I fell backwards into a woodbox, which was just about as wide as I was. Only my feet and head were sticking out, and I couldn't move or free myself. Hugh was pretty mad by this time and stood there whaling away at my face, hitting it through my legs. He kept at it till I could hardly see.

Then I guess he got tired for he went off. I got out and got my eyes opened enough to see John Tonitu, who had come in, give Hugh a good licking.

A few minutes later I saw Hugh in the distance. He was just going into one of the buildings. I called to him, "Hey, wait a minute." He stopped. "Your father is messy around the ankles," I told him, referring to the fact that Old Man Coonie always had something messy or hanging around the ankles. He made a dash at me and we started fighting again. As before, I got the worst of it. Hugh still has a bad temper today. Otherwise he is a fine fellow and one of my best friends.

My sister was there at school too. But I didn't pay much attention to her. She'd try to talk to me, but I'd just go on.

My father came up to school to see me lots of times. When he came I would stay with him.[50]

At this time I began to realize the conflict that existed between Christianity and Indian beliefs. An Indian who has grown up in an Indian background will always have his own beliefs. The old people encouraged us in education. They said the old customs wouldn't help us now, that conditions had changed, and that the new way was necessary to make a living. But when it came to religion it was a different thing.

For the first time in mission school I heard about a heaven, a place above, and about punishment and reward in heaven, and about the necessity to be saved. When we told these things to the old people they said, "That may be all right for the white people, but the Indians are a different race, and set apart, and peculiar, with a religion peculiar to us."

I used to debate with myself for hours. Some of the teachings in school made me think along those lines.[51] I used to wonder who made God, and who was the fellow who made him. I couldn't get it straightened out. The story about Yeye is the Indian main belief of how he came to be, and for years I used to think over these two versions and try to decide which was right.[52]

I could not get myself to accept the Christian idea of hell. It seemed impossible to me that people could believe such a thing. I used to wonder if the people who claimed to believe it were sincere. There was an Indian preacher, Frank Wright.[53] He was a good preacher too. I used to listen to him and wonder if he really could believe what he said.

It seemed to me that I must make a decision. I must decide which religion I was going to believe in. I kept putting it off and off. I did it, but only out of courtesy to the mission teachers and for appearances. In my own mind I still held the old beliefs.

Now I feel that no Indian can escape the beliefs of his kind unless like Dr. Montezuma he knows nothing of them.[54] Old Man Coonie was the biggest Christian among the Indians at Ft. Sill, and was a mighty good man too. But he had many Indian beliefs.[55] When he was sick he had the medicine man, and in his last days he even joined the Silas John Cult.[56]

I used to wonder who had a right to judge me and condemn me for my Indian ways and beliefs. They kept telling me that if I did things the Indian way and thought as an Indian, I would go to hell. But I had not asked to be an Indian. I did not ask to be taught these ways. I could not see why anyone had a right to send me to hell because I had not been trained as a white man. I thought sometimes that maybe someone did have such power, but I couldn't agree that it was right. I wondered what was going to happen to the people who had passed on before me. If someone had the right to judge me. Many of my people had died in ignorance, had not known of the gospel. How were they going to be provided for? I thought about that. If they were going to be punished, they who did not have a chance to choose, I didn't see any chance for myself who knew better, who had heard the teaching, but who couldn't accept. I didn't condemn the teaching, it just confused me. I was like a man standing in a fork of the road, hesitating there and not knowing which way to go. I was a young boy, less than eighteen at this time.

Once at the school, when I was first there, I got baptized with a row of children. It was by my free will. Later these doubts began to creep in.

The Indian is in a peculiar situation. The Indian religion does not try to convert anyone. The Indian believes that a white man can have his own beliefs and be all right. On the other hand, the white man claims that his way is good for all. If the white man is right, the Indian is lost. He must accept the white man's religion. But even if the Indian is right, the white man's religion is enough for the white man. So the white man has the advantage. This is what made me wonder whether it was just, and question who had the right to judge me.

Today I am in no better position. I cannot accept the belief in a hell. On the other hand I cannot believe in the Indian afterworld, where all live as the old-time Indians did. It is still more ridiculous to me. If I must choose between the white religion and the Indian, I choose the white. But it is only intellectual. I cannot agree in spirit with much of it. Some of the people, the younger ones, condemn me for this. "You must believe, you must accept Christianity," they say. "You are lost," John Allard says to me. "You talk like the matron at school used to," I answer him.

I don't know what to believe now. I think the Indian should be educated one way right from the start, or be allowed to have his old beliefs. I guess I'm ready for a new religion.

I can't accept Silas John's religion either. I poke fun at it and a great many people get angry at me for this.

I think the only way to teach an Indian religion is to first know his life, his customs, his beliefs. The old time Indians don't understand the gospel. For appearance he goes to church, perhaps, but he doesn't understand. The Indian by nature is very religious. If a man understands him and knows the customs of the Indian, he could get his teachings through. But he has no knowledge of the customs, of the reactions of the Indian, and he does not inquire.

No one has been able to tell me why a great many things that I believe are not right. Like ghosts, *godlue*, and others. I'm just told that they are wrong. But why? Nobody ever explained. On the other hand, many old people claim that these things are so, and give proof of how they were helped in the old days through these beliefs.

One certain preacher said, "I don't see why these Indians don't take to Christianity. I don't know if I'm no good, or what." That man was the best missionary I ever saw. But that man didn't know the first thing about Indians. There was nothing the matter with the Indians or the man. But he didn't understand the Indians, and the Indians didn't understand him. That's all.

One day a preacher gave a talk on temperance. He said it was a sin to eat too much, or to drink too much. The Indians gathered in a bunch after the sermon and talked. They were saying, "What's the matter with that fellow, what's he talking about?" There is nothing in the Indian religion that has this idea. They couldn't understand.

At school I was pretty scar[d]ey. At night before we went to bed I had to get someone to go with me to the toilet. I was afraid of ghosts. I heard so many ghost stories. That was what the Indians call being influenced by ghosts. If I had been like this in an Indian camp, it would have been a case for a ghost medicine man. But my folks didn't know of my condition and I was at a mission school where it was impossible to have ceremonies. If I had had a ceremony I would have gotten over it at once probably. But as it was it hung on for years. I would wake up in the night screaming and be afraid of the dark. It lasted until I was about twenty. I always had a tendency to look back and see if anyone was following me when out at night. The children did not interpret it in the Apache way, they thought I was a coward. I didn't realize what the matter with me was then, but now as I look back on it I know I must have been suffering from ghosts.[57] I was afraid to go to the laundry alone before it was dawn.

I was afraid most of all of the hospital. I had heard that it was a pretty bad place. Once I was sick and at the hospital. Naiche was sick and was there too. My father came to stay with me and sat talking with Naiche all the time. Those two old men were talking about the dead and about ghosts. My father would say to Naiche, "So and so died right on the spot where you are lying." Naiche would say, "What! so and so, that damn fool, did he die here?" That was an awful thing to do, to call the name of a dead man, especially at night.[58] My father would answer, "Yes, he died right there with a smile on his lips." Those two men were not afraid, but I was just shaking.[59] I thought to myself that they must be very brave. I was scared at the hospital all the time. I think now that it kept me from getting well, for I was there a long time. It seemed like about two or three months. My father stayed with me all the time. It was the army hospital. That night that the old men talked about dead people stands out in my mind. It was such a brave and unusual thing for them to do.

My father was very brave that way. He used to say that he wasn't afraid of any ghost. He used to get disgusted with me because I was so afraid of them and woke him up so much at night. He'd tell me that if I showed them that I wasn't afraid they'd leave me alone. To show me what a good example he was he told me of the time when the window near which he was sleeping opened up by itself and he kept right on sleeping.

I wasn't this way until about seven years old. Then I heard about ghosts and from that time I was pretty afraid.

I broke myself of this later, when I was about eighteen or nineteen and staying with my father at Ft. Sill. It happened this way. We were still living on the reservation, but most of the Chiricahua had gone to Mescalero. An old Mescalero came to visit my father. At the time we were living in a double house. My father had one side and I had the room on the other side of the porch. During the day my father said to me, "Now I want you to let the old man have your room. I've had the house that Ben Astoyah used to stay in cleaned up for you.[60] Your sister has washed it up, put a rug and a good bed and table in, and it will be nice and comfortable for you." As soon as I heard this I began to be scared. The house he was talking about was a double place like ours. It had not been occupied for a couple of years. Before that several people had died in it. It was about one hundred yards from our place and surrounded by a barbed-wire fence. I worried all day. But I was afraid to say anything to my father, for I knew he would kid me about being afraid, and probably get mad at me too. So I just got more and more nervous.

That night we were all in my father's room. The old man was talking about life at Mescalero. My father kept asking him questions about how they lived at Mescalero, and the old man was telling all about the place. It was getting pretty late. By and by my father turned to me and said, "You'd better go over to bed." "Oh no," I said, "I'm not a bit tired. I like to stay and listen to the stories." About a half hour later my father said again, "It's getting pretty late, I guess you'd better go over there." "I'm very much interested in these stories," I told him. "I don't like to go and miss them." All this while I was getting so tired that I could hardly keep awake. I had to force myself to keep from falling asleep.

About twelve o'clock the old man said, "Well, I guess I'll go to bed." This was an invitation for me to go, but I stayed right on. Finally my father was getting pretty irritated and said, "You'd better go over there now. Here are some matches and you'll find the lamp on the table." So I had to go.

I went to the place. As I got in the doorway I quickly lit some matches and lit the lamp as fast as I could. The first thing I did was to throw aside the blankets and make sure there was nothing in the bed. Then I looked under the bed. I took the lamp and looked all around. At the top above the bed, there was an opening for emergency in case of fire. I looked up there. Then I ran over to the other side of the house. It was empty and deserted. All the while my heart was pounding and I was shaking. I didn't go right to bed. I hated to get in that bed. I sat up and tried to read. By this time I was dead tired. After about an hour I just had to go to bed. I crawled into bed, but I put the lamp right where I could reach it. The bed was against the wall and I was lying on my left side.

No sooner did I lie down than I heard a tap, tap, tap under my bed. A cold sweat broke out on me. I grabbed that lamp and looked under the bed. Nothing was there. No sooner did I lay down again than I heard that noise again. I jumped out of bed and grabbed that lamp again. As before I could not see a thing. "I'll be damned if I stay in this place," I thought. Then I considered how my father would laugh at me and tell everyone. I decided that I must have imagined it, and went back to bed. I listened intently and sure enough I heard it once more, louder than ever. I never did know just what I did. I remember that water was streaming down me. My hair felt like it was standing straight up. I grabbed those blankets and the next thing I know I was on the other side of the fence with them. How I got there I never did find out. It was a high barbed-wire fence and built close to the ground. I don't know if I jumped the fence or threw the blankets over and crawled under. All I know is that I showed up at my father's place with the blankets untorn and without a scratch. I must have broken the world's record. When I dashed in my father looked at me in amazement and said, "What in the world are you doing here? I thought you were in that place sleeping" I said to him, "You can go over to that place if you want to, but I'm not going back there." He began to get pretty mad and tried to get me to go back. "Why, you've only been there ten minutes," he said. But I wouldn't go. "All right," he said, "You can stand where you are all night. You're not going to sleep here with me." "Then I'm going in to that old man," I told him. "It's my room anyway." "You leave that old man alone," he told me. But I went in to the old man. "Do you mind if I sleep with you?" I asked. "No, no, come right in," he invited. I told this old man that I came over to get a drink and that I didn't want to go all the way back. But in the morning my father told on me. He kidded me about it for years.

Several years later I was lying in a bed. It was in a place in which I was not afraid. I began to hear that same tap, tap that I had heard in that house. But I was not afraid this time, and just thought it over and tried to analyze the situation. Suddenly the answer came to me. I was lying on my left side and the beating of my heart was making the spring of the mattress move slightly and this made that noise. I was lying just as I was that night, except that my heart was not pounding, and therefore the noise wasn't so great. "What a fool I've made of myself," I thought, "and here I've been kidded by my father all these years on account of this."

One man was telling me that he was coming home from hunting. It was between dark and dawn. He saw two big eyes looking at him. He got pretty scared. He didn't want to shoot at it because he didn't know what it was. So he ran away and approached it from the other side. When he got there he saw that it was a cow. He said that if he had been most Indians he would have run away and said it was a ghost. That's how most of this ghost business turns out. Three-fourths of it is just something natural, if you stay around to find out. Of course there are some experiences with ghosts that are real.

Pancho is the Mexican sheep-herder at my house. He said to me not long ago, "Dan, come over to that house, something is monkeying around. I believe it is a ghost." The roof is of tin and flaps in the wind. I guess he thought it was someone knocking at the door. I just laughed at him. "Oh, I've stayed there a long time," I told him. "I never have been bothered."

Now I always have the same kind of a dream. I find myself on a high cliff, tower or building, always something high. There is a ladder or a pipe—they are always either squeaky or greasy and reach only half way to the ground, and there is no power that can bring me down. I don't fall off. I wake up before that. Sometimes I'll be up there with a group of people, friends that I know. There are no special ones that are there time and again. Sometimes the pipe is just out of reach and I feel like jumping for it.

I have another sensation, but I don't think I am asleep when I have it. I close my eyes and seem to be looking down a vast pit. At the end is water sparkling. If I fall (I am looking over, looking down) there is no hope for me. I think, "What if I fall?" I enjoy the sensation, enjoy the fear. I can take my eyes from it, but don't like to. When I'm afraid it's going to charm me I open my eyes. Sometimes it gets to be a nuisance for it comes back as soon as I close my eyes.

Sometimes when I close my eyes the muscles of my chest and arms seem to swell up like a prizefighter's. They get tense. I almost get afraid. Then I open my eyes.

I knew about the Indian "giver of life" when I was just a tot—five, six or seven. I heard about this first, before I heard of the Christian

God. I just thought of him as one who gives—he was the one who gives. He gives life. He does not make demands of me. He was not going to punish or judge. He did not make out a schedule for me. I was to make requests to him, for he gives life and all good things.

There was no teaching that he made the place below, there was no belief that there was a connection between the "giver of life" and the afterworld. He was free and he left me free. It was just taken for granted that there was an afterworld, and that the Indians would all go there. There was no death there, but lots of good things to eat. Even the whites were mentioned. In the stories people were coming here from white men's towns with good things to eat. People were going hunting. The world goes on just the same, only on a bigger scale and better. There is no more death. They just go on living happily. Life means more. That's what I heard.

I often thought of praying to "giver of life." I prayed mentally. Later on, even when I heard about the Christian God, it was "giver of life" to whom I turned when I was in trouble.

Yet it was a big question for me to decide. There was the white man's religion. They told me that if I didn't accept it I was lost. And the white man had all the proof. He had history to show that Christ was really down here. He had books and writings. The Indian only had his beliefs. It was a pretty serious condition for me to face.

Once I asked a preacher about those who had gone before, in ignorance, about what would become of them. He got mad. I guess he thought I was just trying to act smart, but I was really trying to find out. He just said sharply that for them a way would be provided, but for me it was a different matter, since I was not in ignorance.

The reason it gave me so much trouble at this time was that I was weighing the Indian beliefs with the Christian. I did not know where to go for help. I was in the dark. The missionaries told me that Jesus would help me in everything, to be a better man, that I could be saved through it. But I would have to meet certain conditions, certain things were demanded of me, they said. According to Indian beliefs, "Changing Woman" gave birth to "Child of Water."[61] He had done a great deal for the Indians. He had provided all that was necessary. No demands were made on us. These were the two sets of views that were before me.

The Indian's nature, the life of the old times that they had been telling about, was free. They gave gifts to one another and didn't expect anything in return. If a man liked you he would say, "I am going to give you a horse, or a ring"—like that—free. To give was considered a good trait—to give without return.[62]

Giving is a great thing with the Indians. I don't think there was much selling in the old days. There was lots of giving. Even now there is not much selling. I could walk up to any man and ask for a horse. The less I know him, the better chance I have of getting it. I've been offered horses. Hugh Chee offered me a horse, but I never took it. I did not take it because I did not want to feel under obligation to him, though I am sure that according to the old way of thinking no obligation would be incurred. He just offered it to me to show his friendship. This was practiced in the old days a great deal.[63] A Navaho gave my wife some jewelry. Then he was considered our friend.

Our religion was lined up in that way. That was my teaching.

Then I got Christian influences. Everything was against this way of thought, everything was lined up against it. The bottom was knocked out. If I was to accept this way, nothing was left for me. I couldn't understand that, my background was different. We didn't work for a reward. We expected it. We were made. It was provided for when he made us. The future was already provided for us. We didn't have to worry about that. There was nothing in our hearts and minds that made us worry about it. We just asked "giver of life" for a long life and good things on earth. None of us worried about this till Christian influence came.

Now the Indian's main concern is fear. Fear of hell is what sends them to church. That is why they hold on to the two religions now. They are afraid not to have something firm to have a hold on. I've been thinking a good deal about this. It seems that the whole Indian life is fear. The word is used a great deal too. Fear of eating the head,[64] fear of this and that. I go visiting people and hear it. I don't want to visit that old man Chato.[65] I stood in front of him. He said, "Don't stand over me, someone performed a ceremony over me and said that no one was to stand over me."

Another thing—the older Indians told me at that time that I must accept certain things, that I must put on white men's clothes. In order to live now, they told me, I must try to live on a higher plane. I must try to get an education. On the other hand they taught me all the old beliefs. They would say, "In the old days it was all right, but now times are different, you must get used to the changing conditions." Yet they held on to the old beliefs and they themselves were holding back. Then as I got older I realized that they were right, that I did have to accept the new ways to get along. But this was the problem—was I to accept them entirely? How far must I go? What about the religion? Could I be like a white man in every other way and sit on the fence as far as religion went?

My father used to talk to me. He told me that I must accept certain things if I wanted to or not. "If you don't, it's just like a race, you'll be left behind," he told me. "It's just like a game," he said. "You have to prepare for it." "In the old days any Indian could make a living," he said, "but the younger people who live today must accept education." He was thinking of my preparing for some kind of practical work. He was not thinking of religion.

Only once did he talk to me about religious life. He met me at a camp meeting. He asked if I accepted this religion. I told him that I did not, that I didn't know what to think. "Don't you think you ought to decide?" he asked me. "No, I don't feel that I'm ready to," I said. "I have been baptized and I feel as good as anyone." "Well, it's up to you," he said.

My father defended Christianity all his life. At one time he was very ardent. He used to tell me that I had never really tried Christianity. But toward the last he weakened. He still held on to some Christian beliefs, but he thought he could accept what was good in both religions, and hold to the old and have the new too. I used to tell him that he should be one or the other, that he should accept Christ entirely if at all. But he said that the Indian was a peculiar race, that Christianity had to be modified to suit his need, for he has a different background and cannot understand it in the pure form. "Instead of telling the Indian that it is a sin to wear a feather, or this or that," he would say, "if they pinned a cross on an Indian and let him wear a feather, and put a cloth with some paint on over his shoulder while they taught it, the Indian would take the teaching and take it straight. And the teaching would be the same. The Indian should be approached through his own ideas and ways, instead of telling him to throw them all away and walk the other path. The Indian cannot understand this." And now I believe my father was right.

I used to make it pretty hard for my father. He knew that I was not very ardent about Christianity and always suspected me when I read the Bible to him or something like that. He would often ask me to explain a passage in the Bible, or interpret a sermon for him. I would tell him it said that even if you thought wicked things you were lost. You had to put them out of your mind and heart. He would say, "It does not say that, you are making it up," or, "he never said that." I used to get him pretty well worked up. Sometimes I exaggerated, but usually I reported it pretty well as it was.

One thing I noticed, the Indians felt that the whites considered them an ignorant lot, without principles, or morals, or good conduct. They thought the whites considered themselves the only ones who knew how to live and think right. We thought that you people didn't understand; we had a different moral standard. It satisfied us. That's all we cared about. We weren't trying to convert you to our ways. We thought that we were all right in our way. We gave credit to the whites when it was coming, we realized they had a high civilization.

But the Indians did resent the attitude of the government and missionaries toward his beliefs and ceremonies. The tepee feast is a case in point. It is a religious ceremony, but the agent and missionaries always complain of the expense.[66]

Sam Chino doesn't direct it right at me, but he sometimes says that the young people first cast aside the old religion and damn it without knowing anything about it.[67] He says that it's not foolishness when you study it carefully and see what it means. He feels there is a lot of good in it, and that we younger people are just heading for trouble if we just throw it aside. I believe he expresses the idea of all the old people. They feel that what they stand for is just being shoved aside.

My first *tiswin* party came when I was fourteen. I was attending boarding school then, but it was during the summer. Naiche's wife told me to tell my grandmother to come over that afternoon for they had some *tiswin*.[68] She invited me and John Tonitu too. This was over at her place. She handed me a cup of *tiswin*. I refused it, for at this time I had the Christian religion at school. They told me it was a sin, you know. I went right over to my grandmother and told her. My grandmother asked me if I was going to Naiche's. I told her that I had refused. Then she gave me a good box on the ear, for it is very impolite in the Indian custom to refuse when offered anything. If some one gives you a gift you must take it, so as not to hurt his feelings. I lost my religion right there. I went with them and attended that party.

It is not considered a sin, according to our mind. It is just a social occasion. Some of them got drunk. I drank a lot and got drunk. I was not used to it. They sit around and tell stories at these parties, laughing and talking. A man with a bad temper could not get in. It is considered very impolite to come in on a party without an invitation, but some get around this. When I got drunk it was not considered disgraceful by the old people. I did not get sick. I got to feeling good. It lasted about two hours.

One cup is kept going. The woman who gives the party does the dishing out. A boy of about fourteen can attend. Usually a girl has to be about eighteen or nineteen years old. A sixteen year old girl was the youngest I saw drinking. A man would never make *tiswin*. (Laughter)[69] It would lower his status. My uncle Spitty used to make it, but he was a roughneck and didn't care about his status.[70] He lowered himself many times. (Laughter) After that I attended whenever I could. . . .

All the time I was at school I never did my work outside of actual schoolroom. Home work was assigned and I carried books home, but I never looked at them. I'd throw them under the bed, or something like that. I'd glance through the book five minutes before the class and cram. When it was my turn I stood straight up and talked a whole lot, as though I knew what it was all about. I just hated arithmetic. John Allard did too. When the teacher would say, "Now we will have our arithmetic lesson," John and I used to look at each other and make hateful faces as if to say, "Aw Hell."

Summers I stayed with Bessie. I was always glad when school was out. I would be free to swim and play. I hated school and used to cry when I had to go back.

My visits to Sam Bindi started when I was in mission school. I was about thirteen years old or so. I did this in summer when I was living with Bessie.

Just accidentally I came to him the first time. The children were afraid of him and when I was with them I acted this way too. But really I was curious. I wanted to learn more about this man. So I went up there. I didn't let anyone see me. I went a round about way and came in the back door. I went during the day. The door was open. He told me to come in. He was lying on the bed, singing. He was a middle-aged man then. He was singing a social song. I expected to see something. I expected to find some proof of his witching. But I failed to see anything. He seemed just like a normal man to me that first time, that's what I thought.

He didn't act like he was surprised to see me. He stopped singing, offered me a chair and asked me to sit down. I stayed with him about an hour. I had gone there to see if he acted queer. I had heard so much about him. I didn't see anything suspicious though. When I went I still thought he was a witch, though I had no reason for it. I just thought he hadn't revealed himself. I don't think he suspected the reason for my visit. He just talked on in a social way. I asked him for a smoke several times. He gave it to me. At first when I asked him for a smoke he hesitated. He asked me if I was allowed to smoke. I told him that my Aunt allowed me to smoke. Then he gave it to me. That's one of the reasons I kept coming. It was unusual for an older man to give a boy a smoke. A boy wouldn't ever ask an old Indian for a smoke. He wouldn't dare.

The first few times I went I took pains to be unseen by others when I was visiting him. At first I thought it was something daring to do, but after awhile it wore off. This was after about eight visits. It was about four or five times before I went openly. Later I went openly to visit him. It was known. But I was never called down for it. He has visitors like any other man.

Even after I was visiting him openly myself, I used to avoid him when I was with the other boys.

It was unusual for a young boy to visit an older man like this. On my visits we used to talk about everything. Once when I was older, about eighteen years old, he talked about women. "Do you know this woman, or that woman?" he would say. "Do you think she is beautiful?"

He would ask about one. "I'd like to get that woman for my wife," he said a number of times about one particular woman. She was a Comanche. He danced with her a number of times. Some people used to kid him about it. I don't know if he was serious. I never knew him to be very intimate with any Apache woman. He had a boy, so he must have been married once. I heard that he wanted to get married again, but he was turned down because of his reputation as a witch.

I took precautions while I was going to him though. I was afraid of being witched. I didn't accept anything from him. Once I refused a fifty cent piece, though I needed it badly. I wouldn't eat there either. If offered food I always explained that I had just eaten and wasn't hungry. I did take smokes though. I wanted them pretty badly, I guess, because he could do more harm through smoke than through food, since it is used in ceremonies.

When I first went there I felt that I was doing wrong, but I wanted to see what there was to it. I was getting Christian teaching at the time, but I didn't feel that I was exempt from being witched because of this.

After that first summer I didn't visit him, but I saw him around, working with the other men, and we were good friends then. I never found out why he was suspected, or met anyone whom he was supposed to have harmed.

The children at mission school had a knowledge of the Indian customs. They showed respect to lightning, for instance. When I was about twelve, the boys of my age would put a piece of grass in their caps if it would begin to storm. And they would spit out of respect for the lightning.[71]

We knew that teeth should not be left around where any one would get hold of them, for a witch might get them. Instead they were thrown away where they would be least likely to be found. They were always thrown toward the east. I was warned of this by my elders, especially about the time I was losing my first teeth.

We played Indian ball a great deal at school too.

Once, toward the end of my stay at the mission school, John Allard and I had a dialogue to give. When our turn came and we got up, John was so scared and his face showed it so plainly that I just started laughing and couldn't stop. We tried to start our dialogue several times but I broke out laughing each time. Everyone also began to laugh and finally we had to give it up. John was sure mad at me.

We were frequently punished for all sorts of little offences. Sometimes we had to go to bed without supper. Another way of punishment was to lock us in a dark room. Some boys used to steal cakes and pies from the kitchen. In an effort to stop this they said they were going to dope one pie and put it in with the rest, but I took my chances, and it didn't stop the pie stealing.

Another thing we were punished for was for talking Indian. At school, even in play, we were supposed to talk only English. They felt that we would never learn English unless we spoke it all the time. For speaking Indian we were punished by being made to stand in the corner.

We could sense that the teachers, though they treated us kindly, did not think much of us. You could see that they always had their eye on us, and expected us to slip back from civilization any time we had the chance. We were frequently told that we should not go back to the blanket life.

One instance of this kind stands out in my mind. Once I had been playing until it got pretty late, and I had to make a rush for the mess room in order to get in line in time. I was pretty much messed up, and my hair especially was not combed. I was sitting right across from the teachers' table and I heard them discussing it. One of them said to another, "He will get plenty of chances to go around like that when he gets back to his camp, I don't see why he can't keep himself looking decent here." It made me feel pretty bad. It was in little things like this that the teachers showed that they felt themselves superior. They were not bad, but on the whole I think they could have done better.

With the Agent it was different. He was a military officer who was there to carry out regulations, and did carry out the regulations. His attitude was absolutely impersonal. If we obeyed, everything was all right. You could not see any feeling of superiority or inferiority in his attitude.

At this time I liked several girls. They did not like me, however, because of my rough manners. Not all of the boys were as rough with them as I was. John Allard, for instance, was supposed to have pretty good manners. He had a girl.

Of course we had to do a lot of work around the mission. There was as much actual labor as there was school work. Some of our parents objected to this. They felt that we were being sent to school to learn, and that we should not have to do so much in the way of chores and labor.

Simmons, Bessie's husband, had died. Bessie had married another man, Clemens, so I used to go there week ends and summers.[72]

All the women used to gather Saturdays for provisions. Each family had its tickets and with these they got their rations. Money was issued each fall to families, according to the sale of the tribal cattle. The cattle were herded together, but belonged to individual families.

When I was ten to fifteen years old the boys I went around with often used to have fights with Comanche boys. When we were in swimming and not watching they would come and begin throwing stones at us. We would go out and chase them, and sometimes have a fight.

At the time I stayed with Bessie I used to have arguments with her. She tried to get me to stay home and help around the house, and carry water and wood. I used to tell her that I was too old to do such things, and that it was woman's work. I was seventeen at this time.[73] I was here about two years with Bessie.

Up to this time I did not have any sex life. I was too afraid and timid. Some of the boys used to go in for it strong though. There was one boy named Ozani. He used to go to the prostitutes. He began when he was only sixteen. He used to brag about what he was doing. Later on he died. I think he died from a venereal disease.

I can remember the first time I saw a prostitute. I was walking along the road, going toward the reservation. A couple of women came along in a horse and buggy. They offered to give me a lift so I got in. They seemed just like any other people. Pretty soon we came up to a couple of soldiers. One of them hollered out, "Well, how about it today?" So the girls got out of the buggy, leaving me sitting there. One went with one soldier at one side of the road, and one went with the other soldier on the other side. They didn't seem to be ashamed at all. After awhile they came back. They were fixing their hair and rearranging their clothes.

It was the first time I ever saw anything like this. I had heard about it, but I could hardly believe that it was true. I stayed right in the buggy though, because I wanted to see what they would say, but they acted just like they had before and drove on. When I got back to camp I told the rest of the boys about it. They were pretty excited and asked me why I didn't try.

About this time I was sent to Chilocco, Okla. This was an Indian School near Arkansas City, Kansas. John Allard, Hugh Coonie, John Tonitu and Harry Perico were also there.[74] It was not a religious institution, but was run by the government. It was more of a vocational and agricultural course. What we did was do practical work, like working in the dairy a half day, studying breeds of cows, milking, and the rest of the time doing manual training. The rules were pretty strict. We had to be in bed by nine o'clock.[75]

While I was [t]here I sold cards. I used to buy postal cards and then sell them at a higher price, and I made quite a bit of money that way. The students did not get a chance to go to the city often, and they always could use cards to write home to their families.

But I didn't stay there long. Soon after going there I ran away. I didn't like the place. I had been used to being free, besides I was lonesome. When I ran away I didn't get very far. I just got to the next town. As soon as they missed me they called up the next town and told the police officer to watch out for me. As soon as I got there he took me in custody and brought me back. I got a good lecture when I got back.

While I was at this school most of the Ft. Sill Apaches went to Mescalero. There were only a few people there when I got back.[76]

After I got back, that experience with ghosts I had in that old house took place. I was staying, as I told you, with my father. Bessie had married Old Man Goody.[77]

When I got home that summer I worked around on the reservation. Early in the fall Major Goode sent for me.[78] The boy who had taken care of things for him was getting married, and he needed a boy to look after his horses. I was to stay in a hut near the corrals. I ate at the military mess and got twenty-five dollars a month and board. I was not particularly anxious about doing it, but I could not refuse.

Later I got in a scrape with Major Good. It happened this way. One night I was going home with him from some place. He was driving the horses and buggy. When we got to the reservation boundary he asked me if the gate was open. I thought it was and told him, "Yes, go ahead." So he whipped up the horses and went straight on. As it happened the gate was closed, and the horses ran right into it. I couldn't convince the Major that I hadn't done this on purpose. He said, "All right, you report to me tomorrow." When I reported to him the next day he said he was going to send me to Haskell for punishment. I told the other boys that I wanted to go to Haskell. I did not tell them it was for punishment. Some boys went there from choice.[79]

So in the fall I had to go to Haskell. The only boy from our reservation when I was there was Robert Goody. As I said, I got there in the fall. By November I was pretty well fed up with the place. I was tied down and did not have any freedom. I had to take military training, and things like that. So about November I ran away. I went to Kansas City. Watson Mailo was a boy I knew in Kansas City, and he had said he would take care of me. The day after I got in Kansas City I had a job washing dishes. But they found out where I was and brought me back.

When I was brought back I was sent to the office to talk to the Superintendent. He began bawling me out. It struck me as funny and I began to laugh, and could not stop laughing. So finally he got sore and said, "Well, I was going to let you go with just a lecture, but you think you are so darned funny that I am going to put you in jail." So I had to spend a week in jail.

I stayed at Haskell all that year. While I was there I sold those cards and made a great deal of money on it. I bought them cheap and sold them at high prices. I also used to kill rabbits and sell them to the teachers and white employees around the place. I got fifty cents a rabbit for doing this. I used to make real good money, but I never saved any of it. I spent it on the women. It was at Haskell that I got intimate with girls.

I had my first girl here at Haskell. She was not an Apache. I don't remember what she was.

I had been going around with her quite a lot. I could see she was willing because she would stay out late in the woods with me and would let me talk of such things. I talked about it all I could.

One night when I was out with her we got pretty excited. I handled her quite a bit. She resisted a little but not too much, and finally she let me do it. It didn't last very long. I was just like a bull. I don't know if she enjoyed it. I guess so because she bucked.

After we finished I felt pretty ashamed. I took that girl back. I avoided her for quite a time. Later on I got over it and didn't avoid her, but I never took her out again or did anything to her.

I wasn't afraid that I had got her in trouble. I had only done it to her once. Nothing can come of that. You have to do it to a girl twenty, or even forty times, to have a baby. There are cases where a baby has come sooner, but they are very rare. I believe this today. It is a general Apache belief. I have seen it work out too many times.[80]

For a little while after my first experience I was ashamed and felt that I had done wrong. But this wore off.

Then I met a Shawnee girl and we became pretty good friends. I did it to her regularly. I was not afraid of the consequences, and I didn't withdraw or take any other precautions. I felt that it was her own business and that she should take care of herself. She was the only other girl I had at Haskell, but I had her right along up to the time I left.

I went home in summer, at vacation time, and didn't go back.

At this time, since most of the Chiricahua had gone back to Mescalero, the reservation was broken up and the Apaches were given land outside the reservation. My sister had stayed winter and summer at the mission school. After her school was over she went to work at the hospital. Then she went to live with my father. I didn't see much of her. She married while I was away at Haskell, I believe.[81]

With the other Apaches, I was allotted eighty acres. My land was leased out. My father worked his own. I lived with my father and helped him on his farm. I got about two hundred dollars income from my leased land. Minnie's husband worked her land. He had eighty acres allotted to him, but he leased his. Our farms were located in the general vicinity of Apache, Okla. They were scattered among the farms of the white people. The government had allowed so much money so that land could be bought for us.

3

Vincent Natalish

His Schooling, Life, and Writing

Vincent Natalish was born about 1878. His mother's name was either Zahnah or, possibly, Adjindlae. Alicia Delgadillo gives his father's name as Washington (2013, 190), a son of Victorio, both father and son killed by Mexicans in 1880. Natalish's Warm Springs Apache people were forced from their homes by the federal government to the barren San Carlos reservation in Arizona Territory in 1872, but many of them nonetheless served later as scouts for the United States army to track Geronimo's band of resisters. Like other Apache scouts, despite their service, they were sent as prisoners of war to Florida after Geronimo's surrender in 1886.

Natalish was, as noted in the introduction, one of those taken to Carlisle in 1887 by school superintendent Richard Pratt. A number of those young Apache students became sick and died at the school or succumbed soon after being sent home. Others, as we will see, were sent back to their people by Pratt in 1895, although Vincent Natalish was among those who stayed on at Carlisle, and he graduated in 1899. Unlike most of Carlisle's Apache students, he did not return to Fort Sill or to Arizona Territory upon leaving the school, but moved to New York City, where he worked as a civil engineer. Although he does not seem to have lived on it, he did take an allotment at Fort Sill, as did his son, Vincent Victorio Natalish Jr. Both father and son, Fort Sill Apache tribal historian Michael Darrow informs me, "were considered members of the Fort Sill Apache Tribe" (pers. comm., July 28, 2021).

Unlike Sam Kenoi, Dan Nicholas, and Charlie Smith, so far as I have discovered Vincent Natalish did not serve as consultant to any working anthropologist, nor did he compose a life history. But there is some written record of his life and his thoughts, and I present what I have found, hoping others will seek to supplement what can be heard of the voice of Vincent Natalish Sr., grandson of Victorio.

In the early 1890s George Wratten, officially the Apaches' government interpreter but also a member of their community,[1] learned, as Wratten's son Albert would much later write, that "Apache children were dying at an alarming rate" at Carlisle, and so he composed "letters to people who might take action" (Wratten 1986, 110) and have some of the children sent home. On July 25,1895, George Wratten wrote to Hugh L. Scott, "Captain 7th Cavalry, In charge of Apache Prisoners of War," "on behalf of the parents and relatives of the following named Apache Indian children." Wratten named twelve students attending Carlisle, who, he wrote, were sorely needed at Fort Sill to help support their family members, some of whom, he said, "are very old and have none but these children to depend on for work."[2]

Wratten's letters began an elaborate process up the chain of command whereby Captain Scott, having endorsed the proposal to return the children, forwarded it to two other officers, who, upon their approval, sent it on to General Wesley Merritt, adjutant general of the army. General Merritt then transmitted it to the Office of Indian Affairs in Washington, where the matter rested for the moment with D. M. Browning, commissioner of Indian Affairs. Of the twelve "named Apache Indian children," Vincent Natalish was the last, Wratten spelling his name Nat-tail-et.

Natalish had been taken to Carlisle from Florida before the Apache prisoners of war were moved first to Alabama, and then sent to Fort Sill. His mother had remarried, and although Superintendent Pratt did not prevent students who wished to return home for the summer from doing so, he was pleased to accommodate any who chose not to do so. Thus, in the summer of 1895, I believe that Vincent Natalish, seventeen years old, had probably not yet been to Fort Sill.

Nor had he seen any member of his family for some eight years, with the exception of Gail Marko, his older first cousin—born about

4. Left to right: Charles Istee, Vincent Natalish, and Gail Marko at Carlisle. Studio portrait by John Choate, ca. 1889. Courtesy of the Cumberland County Historical Society. CCHS_PA-CH3-027e.

1866—and Charles Istee, "probably the youngest son of Victorio," born about 1874, whom Delgadillo calls "a cousin of Nahtalish" (2013, 122), both of whom had enrolled with him at Carlisle in April 1887.[3] Neither Marko nor Istee was included on Wratten's list of those needed back home although, as we will see further, both were sent back to Fort Sill by Pratt in 1895. Natalish, whom Wratten had named, nonetheless, as I have said, stayed on to graduate in 1899.

Commissioner Browning sent Wratten's letter to Secretary of the Interior M. Hoke Smith, suggesting that he contact P. H. McCormick, inspector of Indian schools, and that McCormick "be directed to proceed . . . to Carlisle for the purpose of obtaining the wishes of said Apache Indian pupils at Carlisle relative to their return home. That he be directed to personally interview each of these pupils and explain to them that this office is willing to return home such of them as may wish to go, but that those who desire to remain can do so."

Commissioner Browning had earlier forwarded Wratten's letter to Pratt who rapidly—only a week later, on August 17, and, as we will see further, vehemently—expressed his views in no uncertain terms without waiting to learn the desires of the Indian students themselves. Pratt wrote to the commissioner that he did not object to sending a few of the Apache students back to Fort Sill, where, he said, they might serve as interpreters for their people, so that George Wratten might be dismissed from the Indian Service, something he strongly recommended. Aware of Pratt's hostility to both Wratten and his request, the commissioner directed Inspector McCormick "to arrange his interviews with these pupils so as to receive from them an unbiased expression of their wishes in this matter," and to record their responses in writing.

On September 13 and 14, 1895, Inspector McCormick interviewed not only the twelve Apache students Wratten had named as needed at home by their elderly relatives, but all forty of the Apache students then enrolled at Carlisle. Many of them were on outing assignments to local Pennsylvania farms, with the rest in residence at Carlisle—except for one who, as McCormick would find, had run away from the school the previous June. In a letter dated September 22, 1895, McCormick reported to the secretary of the interior that he had found the Apache pupils to be "industrious, honest, and economical, and stand high with employers." He nonetheless made clear that "with few exceptions . . . they are anxious to return to their people."

But, imagining rather fantastically what life must be like at Fort Sill, Inspector McCormick wrote that despite their wishes he could not "conscientiously recommend that they shall be consigned for all time to a life of degradation and filth!" Despite this extraordinary judgment, McCormick did indeed support the idea "that such of those who desire to return to their people"—25 of 40, by my count—"be granted that privilege, with the privilege of returning at the expiration of thirty days to Carlisle . . . and placed in the country to work on farms." If, after the passage of those thirty days, any of the students did not wish to return to school, McCormick recommended that they be given land at Fort Sill "to demonstrate their capacity for self support." He also enclosed a "book," as he called it, in which he had recorded the responses to his questions from each of the Apache students to whom he had spoken, with each student's signature apparently attesting to the accuracy of what was reported. That book provides one more small opening through which we may hear the voices of Apache Indian boarding school students.

Of the twelve Apache students George Wratten had named, McCormick could obtain no response from four: Oliver Bit-Chait, Dexter Loco, and Mabel Nah-rado Kiet, out on farms, or from Duncan Balatchu, the young man who had run away.[4] Of those McCormick did interview, Rachel Tsi-ka-da (Morgan) said that she wished to return to Fort Sill, as did Paul Tee-na-be-Kizen, and Dora Cha-en-dee. Naomi Koh-ten wanted to leave Carlisle but for the San Carlos Agency in Arizona Territory, not for Fort Sill. Lambert Istone expressed his desire to "stay here until next fall," while Clay Domieah wanted "to remain here until next spring and then go home for good." Clement Seanilizay said, "I want to leave school. I don't want to go to Arizona. I want to stay east and strike out for myself," an option that none of the officials had considered. Natalish's cousin, Gail Marko, said, "I want to go to my people," and his uncle, Charles Istee, told Inspector McCormick, "I want to go back to my home where my people are." As for Vincent

Natalish himself, McCormick recorded him as saying, "I will stay at Carlisle school. I have a chance to get an education here and I would like to stay." Written below Natalish's signature—almost surely by Inspector McCormick—are the words: "should stay here, can do well."

Here are the responses from some of the other Apache students: Daklugie, who signs his name Asa D. Geronimo, said that he wished to return to Fort Sill; so, too, did James Kaywaykla, Regis Alchintoyah, Anice Sakieh, and Ramona Chihuahua. Jasper Kanseah initially expressed a desire to go home—then apparently changed his mind. Hugh Chee wanted to leave Carlisle not for Fort Sill but for San Carlos, where he said his family was living. Jason Betzinez, well past thirty at the time, and the oldest of the Apaches at Carlisle, said, "If I could stay until the end of this school year I would prefer it, if they would let me go then. If I am not permitted to go then, I would like to go now." Other responses can be found in the file.

But Pratt, as I have said, had already sent his views to the commissioner without waiting to hear from any of the Indian students named, and in his letter, dated August 17, 1895, he had expressed one of the nastier iterations of his maxim, "Kill the Indian and save the man!" He had written to the commissioner of Indian Affairs, "As it seems to be the settled purpose of the Government to raise still further crops of Indians, and to continue the indurated massing tribal processes, catering to the wishes of the old dominating savage influences among them—which purpose is entirely at variance with my ideas of what is either best or necessary,—I feel that I have no recommendations to make in regard to these young people. I will carry out the directions of the Department, whatever they may be."

On October 19 Commissioner Browning informed Pratt of Inspector McCormick's recommendations based on what he had learned of the students' wishes, and on November 7, 1895, Pratt responded, informing the commissioner of the actions he had taken according to "the directions of the Department." He makes no mention of George Wratten here, nor of the apparent desire of the twelve students Wratten had named to return to Fort Sill. He also makes no reference to Duncan Balatchu, who as noted had run away, nor does he mention Dora Nah-rado Kiet. Another student not named is Vincent Natalish.

Pratt did accede to the wishes many of the Apache students had expressed to Inspector McCormick to leave Carlisle, although by no means to all. He writes that he sent "Chas. Istee" and Gail Marko to Fort Sill, as they had requested, and says of Fred Doaskahda that he "does not want to go west, says he has too good a home to leave." This may or may not be what the young man had told Pratt, but what he had signed his name to in the inspector's book was, "I want to go to my people." Although Paul Teenabikizan is recorded by McCormick as having said, "I want to go home to my people," Pratt decided he would "remain east until June and then go"; in other words, that he would stay at Carlisle for another seven months. Dorothy Naiche, Anice Sakieh, and Viola Zieh had all told McCormick that they wished to go home, but Pratt nonetheless decreed that they "will stay east." Vincent Natalish had told Inspector McCormick that he wanted to stay on at Carlisle, and although Pratt did not refer to that wish in his letter to the commissioner, he did, as we know, keep the young man at the school.

The Carlisle *Red Man* for February–March 1899 reported that the "Twentieth Anniversary and Eleventh Graduating Exercises" of the school had taken place "On Thursday afternoon, March second" (1). Like most schools, Carlisle had held its earliest commencement exercises (1889, 1890, 1891) in the spring, but then for a time (1895, 1897, 1898, 1899, 1910, and 1913) scheduled them in late winter, from the end of February to March or, occasionally, from late March into early April.[5] This may have been in order to allow students and graduates to participate in the graduation ceremonies before they went on "outing" assignments at local farms in time to aid in plowing and sowing. But then the school's final two graduations were once more held later: 1917's graduation took place in late May, and the very last Carlisle commencement took place on June 6, 1918.[6]

In 1899 the *Red Man* reported, "Thirty-three Indian young men and young women, representing seventeen tribes of Indians and fourteen States and Territories of our Union received diplomas for having finished the prescribed course of study at the Carlisle Indian Industrial School" (1).[7] With Superintendent Pratt presiding, "Over two thousand invited guests assembled in the gymnasium" (1). On the platform were a number of distinguished people, among them two of the first Native American doctors in the United States, Dr. Carlos Montezuma and Dr. Charles Alexander Eastman, both with strong ties to Pratt and Carlisle. Also in attendance was Estelle Reel, only the year before—1898—appointed superintendent of Indian schools. All of these luminaries addressed the graduates and their guests: and so did Vincent Natalish, himself one of the graduates. He was, Pratt said, "the first Apache to graduate from the school," and, the *Red Man* reported, his "closing oration . . . appeared to be the most taking one of the day" (1). The *Red Man* printed his talk in full. I do not believe it has appeared in print since, and I give it here in its entirety.

A Plea for Justice and Liberty
By Vincent Natalish, Apache

Centuries ago, there lived a tribe of Indians who wandered about in the wilds of what is now New Mexico and Arizona.[8] They, like the rest of the Indians, supported themselves mostly by hunting.[9]

As far back as we can find any accounts of the Apaches, those who have been among them state that they were a peaceable people.

When the Southern Apaches were dwelling at Pinery Canyon,[10] Arizona in 1874, another tribe of Indians who were on the war path and had stolen some horses, came to their reservation and asked the Apaches to join them in their raids, but my people did not have any sympathy for the renegades.[11] Nevertheless the Apaches were charged with having stolen the horses. Their Agent stated that no Indians had been off the reservation and they were just as peaceable as any Indians under the protection of the United States.[12]

The Agent stated that he had received great assistance from their chief, and the chief and people respected the Agent.

The United States Army physician who was with the Apaches for a time stated, "I have been among nearly all the Indians on the

Pacific coast and I have never seen any, who showed the intelligence, honesty, and desire to learn manifested by the Apaches. I came here greatly prejudiced against them, but now I am compelled to admit that they are honest in their intentions and really desire peace."[13]

Some years ago the Apaches were, and are now called the "terrors of the United States" and "tigers of the human species."[14] What caused it? Was it the Indians' fault? No, the Government sent the Apaches from one place to another until finally in 1876 they were all ordered to move from their homes to San Carlos. They said, "We would rather die here than to live where we do not belong." In spite of their objections the Government attempted the removal. The result was that some of the bands rebelled, and what people would not? Even the wild animal will fight if you try to drive him from his chosen place of abode. This is exactly what the Apaches did; they fought to defend their all. And for this they have been called blood thirsty and savage.

A famous United States scout, Wm. F. Cody, who had been among the Indians for many years in the west said, "In all the battles I have fought against the Indians, I knew that they were in the right and that the Government was in the wrong. When the Government treats the Indians justly there will be no outbreaks."[15]

The removal of the Apaches was the beginning of their outbreaks. In every uprising there always have been many who joined the United States forces and fought against their own people—son against father, brother against brother, trying to conquer those who were on the war path.

I distinctly remember when the last outbreak of my people occurred in 1885 at Fort Apache, Arizona, when Geronimo and his men took up arms and left the reservation.[16] Some of the Apaches enlisted as scouts and fought faithfully with the United States army against Geronimo.

I have an uncle who always fought with the United States forces, although he felt that his people had not been justly treated yet he fought against them.

When Geronimo surrendered and was taken to Florida as a prisoner of war, what happened to those Apaches that were loyal to the Government and fought for it? What reward did they receive? Ah, white man, blush to hear it! After all the hardships the scouts endured while fighting against their own people for the flag which waves so proudly over us, the United States Government sent them and their families into exile, and for thirteen years they have been and are now held as prisoners of war. Think of it, Christian Nation, Christian people! Does not such treatment from a civilized government make the blood boil?

I am personally interested in having the records of the scouts made right for I am a member of one of the families thus unjustly treated.

A senator said one time that the United States never rights a wrong until the people demand it. I ask you to demand that the United States should right the wrongs which have been inflicted upon us. Will this be done soon? I am now ready for citizenship.[17] Must I go to my people and die in captivity or am I to be a man and live among men?

Many people say and even a member of the House of Representatives claims that the Apaches cannot be educated and it is useless to try. This is true in one sense, you cannot educate a race of people when you keep them penned up away from civilization like animals in the Zoological garden.

I believe, if the Government gives us justice, liberty and an equal chance with the rest of the people we will show that we have the capacity for learning and that we need not depend upon the Government for support but we can depend upon ourselves.

I believe you are for the uplifting of our race, so am I; you are for the elevation of man irrespective of color, so am I. Let us, recognizing personal worth and individual effort, join hands and work for the betterment of this glorious country of ours which we love so well.

Three years later, in 1902, Natalish delivered a version of this address to the Brooklyn Indian Association of New York, and, titled "A Plea for the Apaches," it appeared in the *Indian's Friend*, a paper published by the Women's National Indian Association. It was then reprinted in somewhat abridged form in the Carlisle newspaper, the *Red Man and Helper* for June 20, 1902. Natalish had by that time been living in the east 50s in New York, where he was employed as a civil engineer. But it remains an open question where he had obtained his engineering training.

Alicia Delgadillo has written that Natalish "graduated from Yale University, earning a degree in civil engineering" (Delgadillo 2013, 191), and Lionel Larré also claims that he "studied at Yale" (Larré 2012, 602n85). I suspect that both took this information from Natalish's obituary in the *New York Times* for October 6, 1922, which reported that Natalish "was educated at Carlisle and Yale" (19). Delgadillo goes on to say that after his Yale graduation, Natalish "completed course work at the Massachusetts Institute of Technology and Columbia University" (Delgadillo 2013, 191), information she may this time have taken from a brief piece the Carlisle *Arrow* for January 31, 1913, had reprinted from the *New York Herald* (it has a handwritten date of "1913" at the bottom). The *Arrow* reported that "Mr. Natalish is a graduate of the Carlisle School and has also been at the Massachusetts Institute of Technology. He is a civil engineer and is taking a special course at Columbia University" (1).

But in answer to a 1909 Carlisle questionnaire that asked, "Did you attend or graduate from any other schools after leaving Carlisle?" Natalish himself had responded with a single word: "No." It is of course possible that he attended "the Massachusetts Institute of Technology" or took "a special course at Columbia University"—even, I suppose, that he had "graduated from Yale"—sometime after 1909 and before 1913 or 1914, when these newspaper articles appeared.[18] But he said that he was already employed as a civil engineer in 1909, by which time, as he attested, he had not attended any school other than Carlisle. Where, then, did he get his training?

A clipping in Natalish's Carlisle file from the *Brooklyn Eagle*, October 20, 1912, states that he had "studied engineering at *Carlisle*" (my emphasis), and Larré also claims that Carlisle, "from which he graduated in 1899" is where Natalish "was trained to be a civil engineer"

165.

RECORD OF GRADUATES AND RETURNED STUDENTS.

UNITED STATES INDIAN SCHOOL, CARLISLE, PENNSYLVANIA.

Name Vincent Natalish '99

1. Are you married and if so to whom? Johanna Lickeman,

2. What is your present address? 110 East 54th St. N.Y. City.

3. Did you attend or graduate from any other schools after leaving Carlisle? Give names of school and dates if possible. No.

4. What is your present occupation? Salary? Civil Engineering.

5. Do you own your home?

6. What kind of a house is it? Number of rooms?

7. How much property do you possess?

Stock

Land

5. Vincent Natalish's response to the first page of the Carlisle 1909 questionnaire to returned students. National Archives and Records Administration, RG 75, series 1327, box 137, folder 5327. Courtesy Carlisle Indian School Digital Resource Center.

(Larré 2012, 602n95).[19] But Carlisle offered only an eighth or ninth grade education that was unlikely to have included instruction in engineering.[20] How he had obtained the training for employment as a civil engineer remains a mystery.

In his other responses to the lengthy 1909 Carlisle questionnaire, Natalish wrote that he was married to "Johanna Lukeman," and that they lived at "110 East 54th St. N.Y. City." And, as I have said, he replied to the question of whether he had attended any other schools with a simple, "No." He left blank questions about whether he owned his home, how much property he possessed, and whether he had money in the bank. Question 9 asked whether he had been in the government Indian Service, to which he again responded, "No." As for other positions he has held since leaving Carlisle, the answer was "Engineering work since I came to New York."

Question 11 asked, "Have you done anything for the betterment of your people. Write fully." In response, Natalish wrote, "I have tried and still trying to have the U.S. Gov't. to give my people the Apache Indian 'prisoners of war' a permanent home who are now confined on the military reservation at Fort Sill, Okla." The twelfth and last question requests that he "Tell . . . anything else of interest connected with [his] life," and Natalish expands considerably upon what he had just said. He writes:

> My people at Fort Sill, Okla. last winter Jan. 1908 appointed me their representative to have the dark shadow of prisoners of war removed from them and given a home. And not be sent from place to another. The true facts concerning my people, how they fought against their own people for the U.S. Gov't and then were made prisoners of war and how the Peace Commission, composed of the friendly Apaches who went to Washington D.C. at the request of President Grover Cleveland and Commissioner of Indian Affairs on their way home, they were made prisoners of war. I am trying to have things straighten for my people the Apache Indians.

Having come to the bottom of the page, Natalish continued along its left side, "This statement is written by me and it is now in President Roosevelt's hands for justice." He had, that is, sent a letter concerning these matters to Theodore Roosevelt, the president of the United States.

But he had done considerably more than that, and I can describe some of Natalish's work for his People based on John Turcheneske's careful research. Although the Apaches at Fort Sill were indeed considered prisoners of war from the time they were sent there in 1894, at least since 1907, the government had been looking to remove them from Fort Sill, which it wished to—and eventually would—turn into the Field Artillery School of Fire. Toward the end of June 1907, "Major General James Franklin Bell visited Fort Sill" and "advised the Chiricahuas of his intention to . . . prepare plans for permanently removing them elsewhere." He suggested that they "be permitted to examine potential resettlement sites in Arizona or New Mexico" (Turcheneske 1997, 100), because President Roosevelt and the War Department were determined that "the Chiricahuas were not to be allotted at Fort Sill" (101).

Natalish had kept informed of the situation, and on March 7, 1908, he wrote to request "Kansas Senator Charles Curtis's assistance in retaining relief for his people" (Turcheneske 1997, 101). Why would he seek the aid of a senator from Kansas? Most likely because Curtis was a mixed-blood Kaw Indian born in Kansas Territory before it became a state.[21] Natalish also contacted Commissioner of Indian Affairs Francis Leupp, who, Turcheneske writes, "asked him to ascertain their [the Fort Sill Chiricahuas'] desires and to examine possible relocation sites in Arizona" (Turcheneske 1997, 102). Arizonans were violently opposed to the return of the Apaches, but Natalish visited San Carlos nonetheless, only to conclude that there was simply not enough land good for farming there. He visited New Mexico as well, where he also found that "the land and country at Mescalero was worthless for grazing and agriculture" (102). Nonetheless, the following year, 1909, retaining their lands at Fort Sill being no longer an option for the Chiricahuas, Natalish wrote to President Roosevelt on January 7—this may be the letter he is referring to in his Carlisle response—to recommend "the

Chiricahuas' release and their return to southwestern New Mexico" (Turcheneske 1997, 103).

COVID has made it impossible for me to see Natalish's letter in its entirety, so that the following quotations from it once more come from Turcheneske's earlier work. Natalish told Roosevelt that "the beginning of their outbreaks" arose from the Chiricahuas' removal from their homes, reminding him that nonetheless, "many of the Apaches enlisted as scouts and fought faithfully with the United States Army against Geronimo." As we have seen, in spite of their service the United States had "sent them and their families into exile," causing them to suffer the "same penalty as those against whom they had fought." He states that for "twenty-two long years they have been and are now held as prisoners of war" (quotations of Natalish are from Turcheneske 1997, 103), a punishment far greater than that meted out to other Native resisters to the U.S. I do not know whether Vincent Natalish's letter brought a response from the president, but these matters would not be reconciled for several years more.

Natalish's Carlisle files contain a form he filled in on September 5, 1912, of "Proposed Students for Carlisle." He had probably been asked by the school to recruit any Native students he thought might attend, and Natalish was able to name only three: John Allen and Maurice Chatto,[22] Apaches from Fort Sill, and Anna White, a young Iroquois woman living not far from Natalish in New York. Of those he named, Allen was eighteen years old and the other two were seventeen, all of them a bit old to begin at Carlisle, although the school did take young men and women of that age. In any case, there is no record for any one of them at Carlisle, and it is reasonable to assume they did not attend.

An article the Carlisle *Arrow* for January 31, 1913, reprinted from the *New York Herald*, reported:

> New York's only Apache chief, Vincent Natalish, will go to Washington in a few days to plead the cause of his people before members of Congress and endeavor to have lifted from them the load of injustice which he says they bear. He does not wish to return to his Warm

Spring tribe until they are released as prisoners of war. Although they acted as scouts for the United States in the expedition which resulted in the capture of Geronimo, Mr. Natalish declares they were themselves taken prisoners. The tribe is at Fort Sill, Okla., there they have the use of the lands which were ceded by the Comanches. There has been an effort lately to transfer them from this country which has good farming land, to a reservation which is largely desert. Mr. Natalish was chosen chief for the purpose of presenting the case to the Washington authorities. He says that his people prefer to stay near Fort Sill after they have been formally released by the Government. (1)

I suspect that rather than having been chosen "chief," Natalish was more likely simply asked to lead a delegation of Fort Sill Apaches in a meeting with government officials. His relatives and friends may have preferred "to stay near Fort Sill after they have been formally released," but as noted, the majority of the Fort Sill Apaches would choose to leave and settle on the Mescalero Apache Reservation in New Mexico, despite the fact that much of it was indeed "desert." They left Fort Sill on April 2, 1913—either before or after the *Herald*'s article appeared.[23]

At the end of January 1914, Natalish responded to a brief postcard survey he had been sent by Carlisle Superintendent Moses Friedman. He gives for his "Present Address" both the 54th Street address in New York and also "San Carlos, Arizona." For his "Present Occupation," he no longer lists civil engineering but instead writes "Supervisor of Indian Schools." That would mean that he was now an employee of the government Indian Service and that he was, I believe, "Supervisor of Indian Schools" in Arizona, not nationally.

As supervisor of Arizona Indian schools, in 1914 Natalish was at the Fort Apache Agency conducting a census of Apaches living off the reservation. It was in that year as well that he was invited to address the annual meeting of the Society of American Indians on "the situation in Arizona." The 1914 meeting of the SAI was to be held in Madison, Wisconsin. Natalish responded to the invitation saying he would not be able to attend, although he nonetheless wished to address the topic raised. Writing from the "Fort Apache Indian Agency, Whiteriver,

Ariz.," he sent his observations to the SAI on September 22, 1914. His remarks, titled "The Apache Situation," would probably have been read at some point to the attendees; in any case, they were published in the *Quarterly Journal of the Society of American Indians* for 1914, in a section called "The Open Forum." I do not believe they have been reprinted since that time, and I give the full text. Natalish provides a detailed account of the situation of Apache people of the sort not often found in the history books, an account of the Apaches by an Apache. Addressing himself "To the Secretary-Treasurer/*The Society of American Indians/Washington, D.C.*," he writes:

> Dear Mr. Secretary: I am very glad to have your communication of September 1, and note contents. I am sorry that I shall be unable to attend the Conference. You ask for the "situation in Arizona." I am very glad to have this opportunity to submit the following to the Society for careful consideration.

Condition of the Apache Indians off the Reservation

> At Globe, Ariz., the Apache Indians live in tepees on the desert lands outside of the city limits. They have no farms there, and simply live there waiting for some work to turn up in the vicinity. The same condition exists at Miami.[24]
>
> At Wheatfields the Indians live in the tepees on the hilltops. They have no farms there and a number of them work for Chinese farmers. The white community there is prejudiced against the Indians and do not want them to live there.[25]
>
> At Green Back Valley the Indians live in tepees and have no lands of their own. Mr. Packard, who owns most of the valley at this place, told the Indians that if they would clear the land and irrigate they could raise as many crops as they wished. They cleared the land, and after three crops he told them he wanted the land for himself.[26]
>
> At Sallymay there are 30 families living in tepees in a canyon. They have some small patches of corn.
>
> At Gisela there are about 25 families living in teepees. Some of them have small farms. The white people in this vicinity don't want

them. When the cow-boys have their cattle round up they tear down the Indians' fences and turn their cattle into the Indians' corn fields. When the Indians are out hunting their ponies, the cow-boys would draw guns on them even when they are out on the road with their families. They have appealed to the civil authorities, but have received no protection from the cow-boys.

At Angora the Indians had small farms in good condition, but they were driven away by the white men and appealed to the civil authorities, but nothing was done to help them to hold their homes.

At San Pedro Valley, 18 families live in teepees on small farms which the white men have not been able to take away from them. Formerly the Apaches owned the whole valley and used it. The white men have gained possession of about nine-tenths of the land, and continually annoy the Indians by tearing down fences and turning their cattle and horses into the Indians' corn fields.

The old Indians told me that General Crook, in rounding up all the Apaches, told them that if they would help him to get rid of the troublesome Apaches and after settling the troubles they would be allowed to return to their various homes, and live in peace, and that they would not be in need. They said they did their part and nothing has been done by the Government to carry out the promises made to them by General Crook.[27] They have gone back to their various homes and found the white men occupying the old farms, and the only thing for the Indians to do was to pitch their tepees on the hilltops and look at the white men in the valleys deriving the benefits from the farms that were at one time their own.

I was informed by the Indians off the reservation that four Indians were killed by white men, but nothing was done by the civil authorities to punish the murderers. A white man was killed and an Indian was sent to the penitentiary. The Indians claimed that the white men were killed by a Mexican.

At one instance a white man killed an Indian at Globe. The white man fled. An Indian was blamed for the murder and was sent to the penitentiary for life. The white man, who committed the murder, was in California and while he was under the influence of liquor confessed that he killed the Indian at Globe and that an innocent Indian was serving a life term for it. The white man was brought back to Globe, tried, and was released. The innocent Indian was also released.

There ought to be something done to help these Apache Indians off the reservation. They ought to have some protection.

I am informed by the Indian Office that the Government has no jurisdiction over these Indians off the reservation and that they are amenable to the laws of the State. I think this would be true if those Apaches owned farms and lived in houses and [were] citizens, but when they have nothing and simply exist in teepees, I think the Government still has jurisdiction over them.

Thanking you for offering this opportunity to me to present this case to your good offices. I am

Very respectfully,

Vincent Natalish. (246-50)

Quite obviously, Natalish was committed to justice for Arizona Apaches generally, not only for his relatives at Fort Sill.

Although they are not the words of Vincent Natalish, I think it is worth citing what Arthur Parker, editor of the *American Indian Magazine*, the journal of the Society of American Indians, had to say about Natalish in his "Editor's Comment," in 1915.[28] Just after offering words in praise of Dr. Carlos Montezuma, and prior to laudatory notice of John Milton Oskison,[29] Parker said: "And what of Vincent Natalish, grandson of Victorio? Does the bone and sinew of Victorio not know what it is to be an Apache, a hunted warrior, a desperate defender of arid hills called home? Can it be that this Natalish, the engineer, student, gentleman, New York clubman, and structural engineer, does not know the needs of the Apache and of his race in general? What ears are those that are deaf to his appeals?" Of course Natalish's "appeals" on behalf of the Fort Sill Apache prisoners, whether the government had heard them or been "deaf" to them, no longer echoed by the time Parker published; the majority of the Apaches, as noted, had gone to the Mescalero Apache Reservation in New Mexico, and the others had accepted allotments around the Fort Sill Field Artillery School of Fire.[30]

After a congressional investigation into mismanagement at Carlisle, Superintendent Moses Friedman was dismissed in the spring of 1915, and Oscar O. Lipps, a veteran of the Indian school service, was appointed to head the school.[31] Vincent Natalish was still living in New York at the time, although he had moved two blocks north and a bit west, to 68 West 56th Street. On December 14, 1915, he wrote to Lipps as follows:

> Dear Mr. Lipps,
>
> I do not know whether or not you remember meeting me in Washington last fall.
>
> I have a boy age thirteen (13) years and is going to Public school here in the city and does not seem to progress very rapidly. Owing to illness he did not start to go to school until he was eight (8) years old.
>
> My wife died suddenly Oct. 1913 while I was in Arizona for the Bureau and my son has been handicap ever since.
>
> I would like to know from you which would be better for him to attend Carlisle or Chilocco you being familiar with the schools.
>
> I have stayed here in the city on account of the boy. I helped him with his lessons since I came back to the city and have neglected my affairs in Oklahoma.
>
> Hoping to hear from you soon in the premises.
>
> I've planned to leave New York on January 3/16.
>
> Very respectfully,
>
> Vincent Natalish
>
> P.S. Vincent is 13 years old—5 ft-4 inches tall.

Vincent Victorio Natalish Jr. was the only child of Vincent Natalish and his late wife Johanna Lukeman. A clipping in Vincent Sr.'s file—(he seems for a short time to have subscribed to the Luce Press Clipping Bureau, based in New York and Boston, to which several other prominent Carlisle alumni subscribed)—from the *Florida Times Union* of Jacksonville,[32] noted that Vincent Natalish Jr. at the age of nine was already a promising painter in oil and a sculptor. I do not know whether or how far he pursued his artistic inclinations in New York or elsewhere. Both Vincent Sr. and Vincent Jr. received land allotments in Oklahoma, and although the father never lived there, I believe the son did—and both, as I have quoted Fort Sill Apache tribal historian Michael Darrow saying earlier, are considered members of the Fort Sill Apache tribe.

Superintendent Lipps responded to Natalish's letter of inquiry promptly, writing to him on December 17, 1915. Lipps informed him that it was now government policy "that schools like Carlisle and Chilocco are no longer allowed to enroll children less than fourteen years of age and then only when they are accompanied by an older child from the same family." It was his belief, however, "that special authority would be granted by the Office at Washington to effect the enrol[l]ment you desire at either of the schools named." Lipps advised, "As to the selection of a school I must state that your own location for the next year or two should govern that to a great extent. If you intend to locate in Oklahoma it is my advice that you take your boy with you and that you try to enter him in the Chilocco School." Perhaps it was his awareness of the recent death of Natalish's wife that led him to add, "It will mean much to him to be near you and where there will be afforded the opportunity to visit him from time to time while he is in school." He closed by offering his further "assistance . . . in the matter of placing your boy in school."[33]

Wherever Vincent Natalish Jr. spent his next two years at school, he did not attend Chilocco—the index of Chilocco students has no record of him—nor did he go to Carlisle, as we will see further. If Vincent Natalish Sr. had indeed left New York in January 1916 as he had planned, he was back in the city at the same West 56th Street address two years later, and once more considering the possibility of sending his now-eligible son to Carlisle.[34] Natalish wrote to John Francis Jr., the Carlisle Indian School's last superintendent, on May 13, 1918:

> Dear Mr. Francis,
>
> I would like very much for my boy Vincent Jr who is going to 16 years old to enter Carlisle soon. What are the present requirements?
>
> Hoping to hear from you soon.
>
> Rspy
>
> V. Natalish

Natalish once more received a prompt reply, Francis responding on May 20. He offered his thought that "I do not know what better school advantages we could give your son than he could get in New York City," nonetheless assuring Natalish, "I shall be glad to take him if you want to send him here." He invited him to visit Carlisle "and see for yourself what we are doing here now[.] There may be many changes since you were a pupil and I think you would be better satisfied if you could see the school yourself before arranging to send your boy here."[35]

More specifically, Francis suggested that Natalish visit the school at its upcoming Commencement scheduled for the week of June 2, 1918. I do not know whether Vincent Natalish attended that year's Commencement, but it was the last Commencement ever to be held at Carlisle. On September 1, 1918, the American flag was lowered for the last time at the Carlisle Indian Industrial School, which closed for good before Vincent Natalish Jr. could attend.

Vincent Natalish Sr. died in October 1922, at the age of only forty-four and was buried next to his wife in Stockbridge, Massachusetts, where the two had owned a home.

In publishing the boarding school experiences of Sam Kenoi and Dan Nicholas as told in their autobiographies, along with what I have found by and about Vincent Natalish, I continue the project of my previous volume, *Boarding School Voices: Carlisle Indian Students Speak* (Krupat 2021); that is, the project of making available Indigenous voices that have thus far been unheard or very little heard, Indian voices not only *about* but *from* the boarding schools. Others may discover more first-person accounts and thus enrich and, indeed, complicate an understanding of the history of the federal Indian boarding schools, major sites of Native and settler-colonial contact. It is my hope that the texts published here will prove of interest to scholars in a variety of academic fields, to general readers, and in particular, to the descendants of these boarding school students.

Notes

PREFACE

1. Previously, in 1930 or 1931, Smith had worked with Harry Hoijer, who noted that his "principal informant for the Mescalero" texts he published—the first five stories in his book—"was Charles Smith" (Hoijer 1938, 2).

INTRODUCTION

1. Woodward Skinner notes that according to the commandant at Fort Marion, no fewer than 65 of the 82 men he had been sent to hold as prisoners were Apache scouts who had served the United States army (Skinner 1987, 11).
2. Between 1886 and the move to Fort Sill in 1894, 246 of the 519 captives—almost half—died (Thompson 1999, 203). See also Griffin-Pierce 2006 and, for a great many details, Stockel 2000.
3. Contemporary critical consideration of the boarding schools may be said to date from 1928 and what has become known as the Meriam Report, which studied the government Indian schools as part of its examination of federal "Indian Administration" generally. Brewton Berry provided an overview in 1968, as did Margaret Szasz in 1974. Significant subsequent studies are those by Michael Coleman (1993), David Wallace Adams (1995), and Jon Reyhner and Jeanne Elder (2004). The introductions to volumes 1 and 2 of my *Changed Forever* (2018, 2020) also broadly discuss the boarding schools and their cemeteries—containing many more graves than had previously been acknowledged or known. Some of these discoveries have been in the news of late (2021).
4. Genevieve Bell's dissertation is the fullest source for facts, figures, and statistics about Carlisle. See also Fear-Segal (2007), Fear-Segal and Rose (2016), and Witmer (2000) for further information about the school.

5. Skinner reports that Sam Haozous "escaped from being sent to Carlisle when his mother hid him under a barrel until Captain Pratt departed" (Skinner 1987, 161).
6. The Chilocco Indian School opened in northcentral Oklahoma—what was still Indian Territory—in 1884. Like Carlisle, its program consisted of a half-day of academic study and a half-day of work. It was—also like Carlisle and the other off-reservation boarding schools—run on a military model, with much marching and the students, male and female, in uniform. Chilocco graduated its first class in 1894 and closed in 1980. For the Chilocco Indian School see Lomawaima (1994) and Brumley (2010).
7. Haskell opened as the United States Indian Industrial Training Institute, also in 1884. Its name was changed in 1887 to honor U.S. Representative Dudley Haskell, who had been instrumental in bringing the school to Lawrence, Kansas. Since 1993 it has operated as Haskell Indian Nations University. Brenda Child (1998) examined letters from students who attended Haskell (and also the Flandreau Indian school), and Myriam Vuckovic (2008) and Suzanna Buchowska (2016) have also treated Haskell. For the other off-reservation boarding schools, Jon Brudvig (1996) and Donal Lindsey (1995) present materials from the Hampton Institute; Robert Trennert studied the Phoenix school (1988); Sally Hyer has treated the Santa Fe Indian School (1990); John Gram considered the Indian schools in New Mexico (2015), and Sally McBeth has looked at former Indian school students in Oklahoma (1983). For the Rainy Mountain School see Clyde Ellis (1996); Amanda Cobb for the Bloomfield Academy (2000); Diana Bahr (2014), along with Trafzer, Gilbert, and Sisquoc (2012) have gathered material on the Sherman Institute in Riverside, California, and Gilbert (2010) has focused specifically on Sherman's Hopi students. Scott Riney has a study of the Rapid City Indian School (1999), Sarah Shillinger has looked at St. Joseph's Indian School in Wisconsin (2008), and Devon Mihesuah has considered the Cherokee Female Seminary (1993). I have listed only book-length studies here, and by no means all that are available; there are also a great many essays in the relevant journals.
8. In my *Changed Forever*, volume 1, I provide detailed readings of eleven American Indian boarding school autobiographies; volume 2 offers studies of another twenty-one; there are a great many more.
9. See my *For Those Who Come After: A Study of Native American Autobiography*.
10. See Nevins for a cogent distinction between what she calls oral "local" genres and the written "disciplinary" genres into which these narratives are incorporated by those who have collected them and in which they circulate.

11. Among autobiographies by Hopi people, see those by Fred Kabotie, Edmund Nequatewa, Polingaysi Qoyawayma, Helen Sekaquaptewa, Don Talayesva, and Albert Yava, all of which deal extensively with boarding school experiences. For Navajo autobiographies, see Kay Bennett (1964), Bighorse (1990), George P. Lee (1987), Left Handed (Dyk and Dyk 1980), Lucky (Griffen 1992), Frank Mitchell (2003), Rose Mitchell (Mitchell and Frisbie 2001), Old Mexican (Dyk 1964), Son of Old Man Hat (Dyk 1967), and Irene Stewart (1980), along with Broderick Johnson's *Stories of Traditional Navajo Life and Culture*. For a study of these, see volume 1 of my *Changed Forever*.
12. Daklugie is frequently called Asa or Ace in the literature, and many of his Apache contemporaries did refer to him as Asa or Esa. But Daklugie made clear on a number of occasions in interviews with Eve Ball that Asa, the name conferred on him at Carlisle, was a name he had "always hated. . . . It had been forced on me as though I had been an animal" (quoted in Ball et al. 1988, 144). In view of that I refer to him as Daklugie.
13. See volume 1 of my *Changed Forever* for an account of Betzinez and Daklugie. Whatever his expressed opinions of Carlisle were, in 1916 Daklugie applied for his daughters Maude and Sarah to be admitted to the school (Krupat 2018, 334n21).
14. But, as I'll note further, Ball took stenographic notes of the interviews she did, and the ones she typed and transcribed render her consultants' speech very much as I imagine they actually spoke.
15. Nevins makes this assessment in regard to a personal narrative Harry Hoijer was told in the 1930s by Laurence Mithlo (Watson Mithlo's father). Webster (2021) develops closely related matters. I reference Hoijer's work—and Webster's—a little later.
16. The young Harry Hoijer, almost exactly Opler's contemporary, did transcribe a number of oral Coyote stories told in Apache from Sam Kenoi. Hoijer, like Opler in the terms I have cited from Webster, also took a stance "at the water's edge," responding, in Nevins's terms, to the stories he was told as "neutral information" about Apaches without any sense that they were also very much communications "to White people more generally" (Nevins 2013, 98). Opler, who provided notes to Hoijer's publication of these materials as "texts" in 1938, consistent with ethnographic practice at the time, also treated them as "information." But see Webster for a specific account of Kenoi's Coyote stories "as a dialogic interaction between social actors" (1999, 137).

17. Anthony Webster has said that Hoijer, working with Kenoi a bit earlier than Opler, "did not record Kenoi's [Coyote] narratives with sound recording devices" (1999, 138) when he spoke in Apache, and I do not think Opler used any for Kenoi's English narration.
18. This and most of the following information I take from H. David Brumble's indispensable *Annotated Bibliography of American Indian and Eskimo Autobiographies*.
19. See chapter 3, "The Case of Crashing Thunder," in my *For Those Who Come After*, and my "Foreword" to the University of Michigan's 1999 reprint of *Crashing Thunder*.
20. George Spindler, for example, had published *Autobiographic Interviews of Eight Menomini Indian Males* and also *Personal Documents in Menomini Peyotism* in 1957, the same year that Louise Spindler published *Sixty-one Rorschachs and Fifteen Expressive Autobiographic Interviews of Menomini Indian Women*.
21. Harry Mithlo writes that although his father, Watson, gave his date of birth only as a "hot day" in 1886 at Fort Marion (Mithlo 2020, 31), that day eventually came to be specified by the family as July 4—a date also chosen by Jason Betzinez for his birthday. Watson Mithlo's obituary in the *Orlando Sentinel* for July 9, 1993, also gives his birthdate as July 4, but puts it in 1888, not 1886. The Find a Grave website gives his date of birth as April 4, 1892, and places his birth on that date in Florida, in spite of the fact that the Apache prisoners would by then have been moved to Mount Vernon Barracks in Alabama. Alicia Delgadillo reports that Watson Mithlo was born either in "the last days of 1892" or early 1893 (Delgadillo 2013, 97). He had remained in Oklahoma, but he also provided eleven Chiricahua texts to Harry Hoijer (1938, 2).

1. SAM KENOI'S SCHOOL YEARS

1. Ball would have taken the 1881 birthdate from Kenoi himself in an interview she conducted with him dated October 6, 1954. He had said then that he had come in 1913 to Mescalero, where his first wife, Anice, soon died of pneumonia. In 1914 he wished to marry a young Mescalero woman named Sarah, only to have her mother say, "Sam, she only seventeen. Too young for you. And you 33" (Ball et al. 1988, 19). If he were indeed thirty-three in 1914, that would have made his date of birth 1881—a date he probably had given to minimize the age difference between himself and Sarah.
2. Citing C. L. Sonnichsen, Robinson writes that Kenoi was a member of the Indian police at Mescalero "in the early 1880s" (Robinson 2000,

251n23). But Kenoi did not go to Mescalero until 1913, and in the early 1880s he would have been at most seven or eight years old. See note 9 for Sonnichsen's further misinformation as to Sam Kenoi's age.

3. Mr. Chino informed me that "at the time of Sam Chino's death, [he] was a very young child," and so "unable to offer any detailed recollections of [his] grandfather." At his suggestion, I contacted the Historic Preservation Department of the Mescalero Apache Tribe to learn whether there are any other "Kenoi descendants" (Chino, pers. comm., July 28, 2021), but received no response.
4. Sub-Sub-Sub Series 3 of Ball's papers at Brigham Young University, box 6, folder 3, contains what is called the "oral history of Sam Kenoi," and folder 14 in box 4 is also catalogued as containing the "oral history of Sam Chino." As I learned from librarians at the L. Tom Perry Special Collections where the papers are held (pers. comm., September 25, 2021), there are only two pages of difference between them and there is no "oral history" in either, only a typed transcription of an interview and some handwritten notes. It needs to be said that Eve Ball's much-lauded work from perhaps the early 1950s to the 1980s with the Fort Sill Chiricahua prisoners of war who had come to Mescalero is fraught with errors. Her energy, interest, and talent for building relationships with them led to interviews documenting personal and historical experiences from their own perspective, one that might not otherwise have received representation. But Ball's cultural and linguistic ignorance—I feel that is not too strong a word—was enormous. To note only the most egregious of her errors, she titled her most important publication of material from her Apache consultants *Indeh* (Ball et al. 1988), a term which she translated as "the dead." But *indeh*, or *nde* was simply the Apache name for themselves, "the people" in their southern Athapascan language, cognate with Navajo *din'e*, "the people" (see Krupat 2018 and Farrer 1992). And the book itself is very difficult to work with. Under "Kenoi," for example, the index to *Indeh* references only a Belle Kenoi—who turns out to be a Shoshone woman. That index does, however, provide two page references for "Chino, Sam," 247, 285. But on the first of these pages there is a full-page photograph of a (Navajo) woman with no text (Ball et al. 1988, 247), and the second does not mention Sam Chino (285). With no background in these matters, Robinson, who did painstaking work with Ball's papers, at the time unsorted and unarchived, repeats and multiplies her errors—and she cites sources that are also inaccurate, as I have noted and will note further.
5. José Mario is also said to be the father of Sam's brother, John Chino—another name I have seen nowhere else. Robinson's lengthy note quotes

Ball and, as I have said, Sonnichsen (1958) to provide a wealth of misinformation (Robinson 2000).

6. David Fatty had been born about 1856 so that in 1932 he would have been something like seventy-six, not eighty-eight, if Kenoi is at all accurate about his father's age.
7. But it should be noted that Harry Hoijer had referred to David Fatty as "an old Chiricahua shaman" (Hoijer 1938, 2), so that he, too, would have had considerable medicine powers.
8. Apache people avoid speaking the names of the dead, but that can't be the reason Sam Kenoi doesn't name his father because, as noted, he said his father was still alive at the time he worked with Opler. He also said a number of things about his father to Eve Ball in 1954 without naming him, although by that time his father would surely have died.
9. Also written as Ho, Who, or Whoa. Kenoi said that the name "doesn't mean anything. He was called that because he stuttered" (Opler 1938, 367). James Kaywaykla also noted, in Eve Ball's words, that Juh "had an impediment in his speech" (Ball et al. 1988, 126).
10. The Chilocco School Index lists Kenoi's dates of attendance as 1896–1904, which would not alert anyone to the fact that he had spent fourteen months at Carlisle, from September 1899 to November 1900.
11. Anthony Webster explains: "The Foolish People were a group of Apaches who were always doing the opposite of what they should be doing," and he notes that "both Foolish People stories and Coyote stories"—both of which Kenoi narrated to Harry Hoijer and Marvin Opler—"offered Chiricahua Apaches opportunities to comment on their changing circumstances" (Webster 2012, 177).
12. Skinner credits the photo as coming from the "George Wratten Collection," part or all of which had been lent to him. The Wratten Collection is now at the Arizona Historical Society, and I contacted Rachael Black of that society to order a scan of it. But Ms. Black searched the Wratten Collection and did not find it. Either Skinner never returned it or it went astray otherwise, and my scan of a photocopy from Skinner's book was of insufficiently high resolution to reproduce for this book.
13. Robinson quotes Sonnichsen from the same 1958 publication as saying that Kenoi "died in 1958 at about 102" (251n23), which is clearly in error. Sonnichsen observes: "Sam Chino . . . lived at Mescalero in dignity until his recent death at the age of 102" (Sonnichsen 1958, 191).
14. See volume 1 of my *Changed Forever*, in particular xxix–xxx.
15. This is one of the very few section titles in the manuscript, all of which are surely Morris Opler's additions.

16. Anadarko is a little over 40 miles north of Fort Sill. Kenoi may have been attending the Riverside Indian School there.
17. Delgadillo identifies Guy Alonzo as Guy Amardo, a stepson of Geronimo, and gives his date of birth as perhaps 1875; she gives December 11, 1895 (Delgadillo 2013, 6) as the date of his death, midway through the first year he and Kenoi were at Chilocco. She reports Henry Yahbecothlay's death as 1899 (Delgadillo 2013, 268). He appears as a student named Henry Yabacola on the Chilocco roll for 1897.
18. Arnold Kinzhuna was one of the Apache scouts who served with the U.S. 6th Cavalry in tracking Geronimo in 1886. He entered Carlisle in 1887 at the age of twenty-one, along with his wife, Hulda Kinzhuna (discussed later), who was then eighteen. I have found no record of his nephew, Henry.
19. A hack, short for "hackney," is a sturdy horse-drawn coach, often used, as here, for taxi service. Chilocco's military regime had the boys wearing soldiers' uniforms and doing a considerable amount of marching and drilling. Girls all wore the same standardized American Victorian dress as their uniform.
20. If Kenoi's birthdate was about 1875, as he stated, and if, as he says, Henry is older, they would hardly have been just "boys" in 1896.
21. It is Opler who was responsible for the paragraphing, and here, as occasionally elsewhere, he may have used short paragraphs to represent brief pauses or shifts in oral narration. But Opler seems to have been little interested in matters of performance, and largely unaware of his status as (part of?) Kenoi's audience.
22. That a white girl would choose an Indian boy she had just met for a sexual encounter—her first, from Kenoi's description of having "ripped something in there," although she seems quite experienced—and then bring him home to her mother and father for tea, is, to state the obvious, not in accord with most descriptions of Indian-white relations at the time.
23. This is Regis Alchintoyah, born in 1877. He had not gone to Alabama because, with Vincent Natalish and a great many other young Apaches, he "had been taken right to school" from Florida in 1887. According to his file, Alchintoyah was a student at Carlisle from 1887 to 1895, when, with a number of other Fort Sill Apache students, he was sent home by Pratt (see chap. 3). Carlisle provided at most a ninth-grade education, so that he was by no means "a college boy." Nonetheless, regarding Carlisle's reputation, Estelle Brown, a teacher at federal Indian boarding schools less prestigious than Carlisle, wrote that, "For an Indian to say that he was a graduate of Carlisle was, in the Indian Service, equivalent to a

degree from Harvard" (207). Thus, Regis, as "a college boy," thinks very well of himself. But as a Chilocco student, Kenoi is also an Indian school "college boy."

24. As noted, Regis had been sent home from Carlisle to Fort Sill in 1895.
25. In Apache matrilineal society, after his mother's death Kenoi would live with his mother's sister, and she would "bring him up." He makes no mention of Carl Mangas, who also played a part in raising him.
26. His Carlisle student information card says that Regis left the school in 1895, as noted. There is no student record for David Kaje or Kazhe, but a letter by Superintendent Pratt to the Commissioner of Indian Affairs dated November 7, 1895, lists David Kazhe as one of the students he sent back to Fort Sill that year. So, too, does Pratt name Charlie Istee—whom Delgadillo believes was probably "the youngest son of Victorio" (Delgadillo 2013, 122)—as having been sent back home in 1895.
27. Kenoi cannot know these things from direct observation because he did not attend Carlisle until 1899. He may, of course, have heard Regis and the others speak of them, and he may have learned these things from his wife, Anice Sakieh, whose time at the school overlapped that of Regis and his friends.
28. Richard Inick has a Carlisle student file under the name Richard Imach, and it records that he entered at the age of seventeen, in September 1899, the same time that Sam Kenoi did. Tom Duffy appears as Thomas Duffet. He also came to the school in September 1899, at the age of sixteen, and would be sent home for "ill health" two months later. Laura and Juanita Parker, Kenoi says, were "Corner Parker's daughters." They were, that is, the daughters of Quanah Parker, a principal chief of the Comanches, who had made Comanche land available to the Apaches to occupy at Fort Sill. Laura Neda Parker (on some records listed as Laura Needle Parker), the older of the two, first entered the school at the age of twelve with her sister, not "Juanita," but Wanada Parker, in 1894. (Wanada was initially registered as Juanada, the school mistaking her name as Spanish. Subsequent records correct that.) Wanada Parker went home for summer vacations and finally left Carlisle in 1901, and she is listed as attending Chilocco in 1902. So did Laura Parker leave in the summers, returning, and finally departing the school in 1902, having reached the ninth grade. But she had indeed reentered the school in September 1899, when Sam Kenoi enrolled.
29. As several times noted, he entered Carlisle in September 1899.
30. An important element of a Carlisle education was the "outing" program in which students were "outed"—sent out—to family farms in the area to work. The aim was to give the Indians practice using English, to have

them learn agricultural or domestic skills, and to allow them to earn enough to appreciate the sound of a few coins jingling in their trouser or apron pockets. As Kenoi correctly notes a little later, a student could refuse an outing assignment if he or she did not wish to go, although pressure from the school might, on occasion, be intense. The students provided cheap labor to their employers, but a considerable number of students wrote positively of their outing experiences. From the overcrowding Kenoi describes, it may be that on this occasion students who were willing to go were sent to farm families simply to house them. Because some students remained on outing assignments during the school year and attended local public schools, it is possible for a student enrolled at Carlisle from—say—1895 to 1899 actually to have spent only a year or two at the school itself.

31. Once again, if Kenoi's birthdate was 1875, this would make him a second grader at Carlisle at the age of twenty-four; a later birthdate would still have him at least nineteen years old. Young people well past the typical age of first or second graders were indeed sometimes at that level in the Indian schools, although to have a student aged nineteen—or twenty-four—in the early grades was unusual.
32. This is Tullytown, Pennsylvania, about 140 miles east of Carlisle.
33. Students were encouraged to call Captain Pratt their "school father"—a gesture of patriarchal colonialism, on the one hand, but also an acknowledgment of the importance of Native kin relationships—and to call the male head of household at their outing farm their "country father."
34. Carlisle files record that Kenoi worked for C. Henson from May 1900 to July of that year, barely three months, and not, as Kenoi says below, two years.
35. Penns Manor, Pennsylvania, is more than 280 miles west of Tullytown, so Kenoi probably means Pennsbury Manor, Pennsylvania, about 4 miles to the west of Tullytown. The Carlisle outing record has him working for Henson in Tullytown.
36. If the Carlisle record is correct and Kenoi got to Henson's farm in May, he could only have gone to the local school for a month or two before summer break.
37. These would seem to be the names of places where Indians were mistreated. But I have found no places in present-day Oklahoma—my guess was that Kenoi was referring to the Fort Sill area—called Whitetail or Morris.
38. He is again using 1875 for his date of birth.
39. Sent to Carlisle—where it was to be held for the student's later use.
40. *The Indian Helper* was a Carlisle newspaper published weekly from 1885 to 1900. *The Arrow* was published weekly at the school from 1904 to

1908, so Kenoi could not have received it at the time of his outing in 1900. The papers published notes on students' activities, sometimes, for example, printing a letter to the school describing the experiences of a student on an extended outing like Kenoi.

41. If the three Indian girls "were just like white girls," that would suggest they, too, had attended the American schools. But Lizzy Chab and Mary Mackay (or McKay) were not Carlisle students; at least there are no student records for them. There is, however, a Carlisle student record for a young woman named Charlotte Bigtree, who attended the school from 1897 to 1904, the right time period. Carlisle's Charlotte Bigtree was a St. Regis Mohawk from New York and not an Oneida, so either this is a different Charlotte Bigtree or Kenoi has assigned her to the wrong Nation of the Iroquois Confederacy. If Kenoi "fought over that C[h]arlotte right in the school," that would have been the "public school or high school" he said he attended.
42. As noted, Kenoi left Henson in July 1900, when Carlisle was not in session. It is unclear why he was not allowed, as he says, to return when school reopened in September that year, instead of being sent out on another outing. This time he is sent to the farm of F. N. Ely of Taylorsville, Pennsylvania, about 10 miles west of Trenton, New Jersey.
43. Carlisle, in Pennsylvania, is almost 150 miles west of Trenton—nor is there any Carlisle, New Jersey, "six miles above Trenton" (18).
44. That is, separate the cream from the milk by skimming it off the top.
45. Duncan Balatchu came to Carlisle in November 1886, when he was about sixteen, and ran away from the school in June 1895. Earlier, from April to September 1893, he had had an outing assignment working for J. Peck of Tullytown, who is probably Kenoi's "George Peak." He would marry Kenoi's half-sister, Daisy Fatty, and later, in the 1930s, work with both Opler and Harry Hoijer (Delgadillo 2013, 13). Charlie Istee had attended Carlisle from April 1887 until November 1895. There is no Carlisle record of him having worked for Peck, although he had worked in nearby Fallsington for Dr. J. Richards from September 1891 until September of 1893, and then again for a year from September 1894 to September 1895. He also appears on the Chilocco rolls for 1897, and there, too, it is noted that he "Deserted" the school.
46. All the boarding schools had one or more disciplinarians. Some were white, some Indian, and the nature and severity of the discipline meted out varied a good deal. When Kenoi returned to Chilocco, as noted, he was given the job of assistant disciplinarian (Kenoi 193?, ms. 45).

47. This is once more confusing. On his arrival a year earlier, in September 1899, Kenoi had told those in charge that he had been in the second grade at Chilocco, despite the fact, as he says, that he had actually been in the seventh grade. Now he says that although he had been in the eighth grade—surely at Chilocco—he claims only to have been in the third grade. The few records on file for him do not list the grade to which he was assigned. If he was indeed placed in third grade, he may have advanced a grade each day because it was apparent that he could speak, read, and write English at a level well beyond that of third and fourth grade. The daily promotion would not have gone beyond fourth grade, however, if, as he soon says, he "had only four more grades to go through to graduate," through the eighth grade, the highest level of Carlisle at the time.
48. Kenoi says he got the letter informing him of his (half-)sister's death upon his return to Carlisle in September 1900. But the date Daisy Fatty died has been precisely recorded. It was "October 30, 1899" (Delgadillo 2013, 83), about a month after Kenoi first arrived at Carlisle, and almost a year earlier than he now says he learned of it. Kenoi did not run away from Carlisle until November 1900. Delgadillo writes that Kenoi as a child at school in Alabama "always defended his sister" (2013, 151).
49. The Carlisle Band was world renowned. If Kenoi is in his "band uniform," he must have been a member of the band, although he does not say—nor have I discovered—what instrument he played.
50. Hagerstown is a little over 50 miles south of Carlisle, so that would have been a long and vigorous night's walk.
51. This is Dr. Carlos Montezuma, a Yavapai, and one of the first Native American physicians, receiving his license to practice in 1889. He had become friendly with Richard Pratt and served as Carlisle school physician in 1893–96, leaving to establish a private practice in Chicago.
52. Telephone service in Chicago began in 1878. By 1900, when Kenoi arrived, there were almost thirty-five thousand telephones in Chicago.
53. Kenoi recalls Montezuma's visiting Carlisle twice during his own time there and seeking out "the Apache boys," perhaps because Yavapai people at the time were usually considered to be Tonto or Mojave Apaches. Kenoi's is the only account I know of a visit to Montezuma's Chicago office.
54. Probably Jasper Kanseah, a nephew of Geronimo's, and a few years younger than Kenoi. He had also been at Fort Marion, from which he had been sent to Carlisle in November 1886, remaining until 1895. Upon leaving the school, he returned to Fort Sill and "served in the Detach-

ment of Scouts," later moving to Mescalero, where he was "a tribal policeman" (Delgadillo 2013, 141).

55. Carlisle and the Indian schools generally did not seek to prepare their students for the professions, but rather for farming, skilled labor, or domestic work. Yet a number of Carlisle students became educators, doctors, dentists, ministers, and lawyers.
56. Republican President William McKinley was running for reelection in 1900 against the Democrat he had beaten in the previous election, William Jennings Bryan. He would defeat Bryan again, only to be assassinated six months into his second term.
57. Haskell is about 153 miles to the northeast of Newton, where Kenoi is now.
58. The November 1909 issue of Chilocco's *Indian School Journal* noted that Gertrude Esau, a Pawnee, was a 1901 graduate of the school (5). That would mean she hadn't yet graduated when Kenoi encountered her working in Guthrie. A Joseph Esau is also on the Chilocco rolls, and James Murie is listed as the father of both Joseph and Gertrude Esau. Murie, a graduate of the Hampton Institute, was a prominent Pawnee leader, and would become an important Native ethnographer. He had married Mary Esau, a Pawnee woman, in 1887. But according to the 1907 Pawnee Census Roll, the two Esau children were born in 1881 (Gertrude) and 1886 (Joseph), before Mary Esau married James Murie. If the Chilocco recorder was correct in listing Murie as their father, they would, then, have been Mary Esau's children, whom Murie—perhaps—adopted after the two were married, although they did not take his name. I'll mention Joe Esau again later, although neither Gerty nor Sam Kenoi speaks of him.
59. I have found no references to a Juanita College. This may be a typo for Juniata College, a co-ed vocational school founded in Pennsylvania in 1876.
60. What Kenoi refers to as a "Comanche school" about 2 miles away from Fort Sill is the Fort Sill Indian School, founded as a Quaker institution in 1871, but nonsectarian since 1891. There also was a Dutch Reformed Church mission school on the post at Fort Sill that had opened in 1899, which, as we will see, Dan Nicholas also attended.
61. Kenoi had had a ticket from Arkansas City, Kansas, where he worked for Jim Ray, to Oklahoma City, about 90 miles north of Fort Sill, and Oklahoma City had earlier seemed to be his final destination. When the train stopped at Guthrie, some 33 miles north of Oklahoma City, he let Gerty cash in his ticket so that he could stay with her. Ponca City is 75 miles

north of Guthrie, so that travel there would take him away from both Oklahoma City and Fort Sill. In saying, "I could have my ticket bought to Ponca City," he may simply be trying to dissuade Gerty from trying to accompany him home.

62. Peyote buttons are to be found in northern Mexico, and the peoples of the southern plains obtained them first from Lipan Apaches about 1880. It's not clear who first brought peyote use to the Pawnee. Alexander Lesser wrote that it was Frank White, a Pawnee Ghost Dance leader, who introduced it into the Pawnee practice of the Ghost Dance (Lesser 1969, 60). Weston LaBarre thought Eagle Flying Above was possibly the initiator, having learned of peyote use "about 1890 or a little later" (LaBarre 1989, 118), just about the same time as Frank White. Gerty Esau is speaking of Pawnee peyote use toward the end of 1899.

63. Although the words of both speakers in these lengthy dialogues are put in quotation marks, they are only Sam Kenoi's best recollections—in Morris Opler's rendering—of conversations thirty years earlier.

64. The Miller Brothers' 101 Ranch was established in the early 1890s in Indian Territory and came to comprise over one hundred thousand acres. The 101 Ranch Wild West Show was first presented in 1905, and on its opening day featured among its attractions Buffalo Bill Cody and Geronimo. The November 1909 issue of Chilocco's *Indian School Journal* reported that Gerty Esau was married to William Perry, a proprietor of a meat market, and that she and her husband were living on her allotment in Skedee, Oklahoma, about 65 miles south of Chilocco. I don't know if Perry was "short," or if despite having been born in Indiana, he had become an Oklahoma champion rider. He had also been a Chilocco student, but he probably was a white man, as Kenoi said. On the Chilocco student rolls, the box to record Perry's "Nation" has been left blank, perhaps indicative of the fact that he was not Native. A Gertrude E. Perry, age twenty-six, is listed on the 1907 Pawnee Census Roll along with the names of her three children, but there is no William Perry enrolled, again probably because he was not Indian. J. J. Farris, in a January 1938 interview, said that "at that time [early twentieth century] Indians and whites alike attended [Chilocco] though now only Indians attend" (quoted in LaVere 1998, 155). Farris himself was white, had attended Chilocco, and was a friend of his fellow student, Joe Esau. He was also the admirer of another student, Hester Parker, sister of Laura and Wanada Parker. In January 1909, the *Native American* published by the Phoenix Indian School announced the arrival in Phoenix of Gertrude Esau and her husband, William Perry. There he would operate

a grocery store, where, in 1926, he was shot and killed in an attempted robbery. Gerty outlived him by fifty years, dying in Phoenix in 1976.

65. He could be referring to David Fatty, his stepfather; or he could again be referencing his biological father, who was still alive at the time his mother married Fatty. It is far more likely, however, that his "father" here is Carl Mangas, who "raised" him, because Kenoi says: "My father had a village." In Jason Betzinez's list of the twelve Apache villages at Fort Sill set up by George Wratten, only Carl Mangas's is among them (Betzinez 1988, 167), and there is no village for David Fatty. Harry Mithlo has his father, Watson Mithlo, say, "Eventually, twelve family groups of Apaches resided at Fort Sill in twelve separate villages or 'clusters,' each cluster presided over by a headman" (Mithlo and Beasley 2020, 59). He, too, gives the names of the twelve headmen of these villages (128), and he differs from Betzinez in only one instance: Betzinez assigns a village to Charles Martine, "a few hundred yards north of Geronimo's" (Betzinez 1988, 167), while Mithlo does not name Martine, and instead lists "Kayiah" (Mithlo and Beasley 2020, 128) as a village headman. But he, too, assigns a village to Mangas and not to Fatty.
66. This would be his Carlisle band uniform, the first time he has mentioned having it since leaving the school.
67. The Apaches shared with other southwestern tribal nations what Michael Hittman has called "ghost fright" (1997, 180). This involved ritual avoidance of the dead and their possessions, including their dwelling places, which were often burned down, as here.
68. This is David Fatty's second wife, Nahdaiyah (Delgadillo 2013, 84) with whom he had a number of children (all named Fatty).
69. Both Hugh Chee, about Sam Kenoi's age, and Kaitah (Kayitah, Kateah), roughly twenty years older, had been prisoners with Kenoi at Fort Marion. Kaitah had been one of the Apache scouts serving with the 6th Cavalry tracking Geronimo, and he, along with Martine—we will hear of him further—eventually urged Geronimo to surrender to General Crook in 1886. Nonetheless, Kaitah, along with other Apache scouts, was sent to Fort Marion and incarcerated. Hugh Chee went to Carlisle from Fort Marion, arriving at the school in 1886 and not leaving until 1896, three years before Kenoi arrived.
70. That Sam Kenoi lives in his dead aunt's house, uses her things, and works her fields, is either very bold or very foolish, or possibly both. Opler quoted an Apache consultant as saying, "people don't want anything that the dead person had used . . . to be around . . . they fear that the ghost of the person who owned the article will come back to molest the

one who keeps it. . . . If a woman's baskets or pots are not buried with her, they put holes through them. Nothing is left whole, for they don't want them used again, even by mistake" (Opler 1941, 474).

71. Dexter Loco, about age twenty-one, was among the first Apaches sent to Carlisle by order of General Crook from the San Carlos reservation in January 1884. One of twenty-two western Apaches, the sons and daughters "of chiefs and important headmen" (Delgadillo 2013, 162), he was enrolled at the school in February of that year. He left and reentered several times and finally departed in 1893. James Russell is probably the man also known as Russell Nadagar, and the brother of Tom Duffy (Thomas Duffet). Alicia Delgadillo notes that he was surely literate (225), although I have found no record of his having attended boarding school. Kenoi simply mentions Geronimo's name here, although he had a violently negative opinion of him, referring to him elsewhere as "an old trouble maker . . . as cowardly as a coyote" (Opler 1938, 367). As for Perico, Kenoi thought of him as "a brave man and . . . one of the best Apache fighters" (Opler 1938, 367). Delgadillo says that his son, Harry Perico, "in 1918 . . . wrote a brief autobiography" (Delgadillo 2013, 221) that she says is in the "Field Artillery and Fort Sill Museum" (315n9). But Robert Anderson Jr. of the museum informed me that although it may exist, he was "unable to locate the Harry Perico autobiography" (pers. comm., July 24, 2020). Benedict is probably Benedict Jozhe, about the same age as Kenoi, who had come to Carlisle from Florida with a great many Apache students in April 1887. He remained at the school until 1899, leaving just before Kenoi arrived. I have not been able to identify Old Paul.

72. Kenoi didn't get to Fort Sill until 1894, so again if his birthdate was 1875, as he gave it, he was not "a little boy" when he planted the peach trees. Thinking of that time now, in the spring of 1901, he is conveying his sense that it feels like long ago, an event from his childhood.

73. Opler quoted another consultant as follows: "Following a death we move camp. The relatives don't want to live in the same place. It doesn't matter whether the person died in the home or not. It is destroyed anyway. Usually it is burned. And they do not go back around that old camp site much either" (1941, 475). In the right hand margin at this point in the Kenoi typescript there is a vertical line, and to its right, the word "ghost" is hand-written.

74. The Pan-American Exposition in Buffalo, New York, was open from May until November 1901. Regis had been among a party of Fort Sill Apaches who had visited, as had Geronimo. The exposition attracted

people from all over the U.S. and the world, and it was there that President William McKinley was shot on September 6, dying eight days later.

75. In the introduction to the other autobiographical account from Sam Kenoi Opler published, "A Description of a Tonkawa Peyote Meeting Held in 1902," he wrote that although Kenoi's "words have not been changed, this section has been greatly condensed" (Opler 1939, 433). It was not only "condensed" but also edited, with spelling and punctuation standardized.
76. Anice Sakieh Kenoi had had two sons by a prior marriage, and she and Sam Kenoi had two children of their own. I don't know the ages any of her children would have been in 1910, but it would appear that she is thinking of sending one or more of them to Carlisle.
77. She has placed Fort Sill in Oklahoma Territory, although the territory had become a state in 1907.
78. This is Samuel McGowan, who had formerly been superintendent of the Phoenix Indian School. McGowan would serve as assistant to the director of the anthropology exhibits at the Louisiana Purchase Exposition in St. Louis in 1904, also known as the St. Louis World's Fair.
79. This may be Bruce Kachenay from Fort Sill, who is on record as having attended Chilocco in 1903. Delgadillo references a Bruce Kaahtenay (1890–1910), who appears in the Chilocco Index as having attended the school from 1904 to 1906 (Delgadillo 2013, 138). This Bruce is also from Fort Sill, but the Chilocco roll gives his tribal affiliation as Comanche. I think Bruce Kachenay and Bruce Kaatenay are the same Bruce, that he was an Apache, and perhaps the one whose name Morris Opler has spelled Kaedine.
80. This is another considerable distance on horseback; from Colony to Blackwell, Oklahoma, is some 180 miles.
81. Both Peter Gaines and George Peso were Apaches from Mescalero, New Mexico, and they are recorded as having entered Chilocco in 1906.
82. At this time alumni were allowed to play on a school's team, as Kenoi and other "old students" played for the Chilocco team. Jeffrey Powers-Beck notes that so far as Indian baseball was concerned, at this time, "the major baseball power in the Southwest [*sic*] was Chilocco" (Powers-Beck 2004, 13).
83. Kenoi had earlier said he'd been at Chilocco in 1895–98. Although he met Sam Morris and Joe Teabo at Chilocco, the two were primarily associated with the Chemawa Indian School in Salem, Oregon, the second federal Indian boarding school to be established. The *Indian's Friend* for December 1903, published by the Women's National Indian Association,

noted that Morris, a Nez Percé, had "won great laurels on the Pacific Coast as a baseball pitcher," and would earn $200 a month (about $5,788 in 2020 dollars) with the minor league Portland Browns (*Indian's Friend* 1903, 8). Teabo, from the Grand Ronde Reservation in western Oregon, would also sign a minor league contract (Powers-Beck 2004, 13). Sam Horsechief, born in 1877, appears on the 1914 Pawnee Census Roll as chief of police at Pawnee, Oklahoma, near the end of World War I. I have found no further information about his participation in baseball.

84. This would be Charles Martine Jr., born about 1886. The son of a man named Chinchee (Delgadillo 2013, 173), he was adopted by Charles Martine and named after his stepfather, who, as noted, had been involved in arranging Geronimo's surrender. Martine Jr. "had attended the Reformed Church mission school on the post for a year and the public school in Anadarko for a year," going on to study "horticulture for six years at Chilocco," from 1902 to 1908. He later continued his education at the Hampton Institute in Virginia, at which he "was enrolled on November 11, 1911" (Delgadillo 2013, 173), leaving in 1916 (Brudvig 1994; 1996). (A brother or half-brother, Dewey Martine, whose name does not appear in Delgadillo's study, is also listed as a Hampton student, entering in 1905 and expelled the following year "for drinking alcohol" (Brudvig 1994; 1996)). The Chilocco *Indian School Journal* for November 1906 reported that Martine Jr. was a member of "The Southern Tribes Track Team"—captained by Joe Esau! They competed against "The Northern Tribes Team," and Martine won the Running Broad Jump (*Indian School Journal* 1906, 29).
85. This is probably young Jim Bluejacket, a Cherokee, not a Kaw. See note 90 following.
86. Martine was, however, a good athlete, as already noted. Duffy, who had entered Carlisle with Kenoi in September 1899, and had been sent home for ill health only a couple of months later, is here clearly recovered and a good baseball player. He attended Chilocco in 1902–8 and was also on the 1906 "Southern Tribes Team," captained by Joe Esau. At the end of his narrative, Sam Kenoi calls him the "best at pole vault."
87. I believe he means that because the government paid for the Indian students at Chilocco, anyone on the team could be considered supported by the government.
88. There is no record of a Rudy Santefugas at Chilocco.
89. Again, if his date of birth was 1875, he would hardly have been a "kid" too young to play baseball in 1895.
90. Jim Bluejacket, a Cherokee, was born William Lincoln Smith in 1887, in Adair, Indian Territory. He attended the Cherokee Male Academy and

played with many teams before being taken on, at the age of twenty-seven, by the Brooklyn Tip-Tops of the short-lived (1914–15) Federal League. This was a professional league, and was or was not—the matter is in some dispute among baseball historians—a major league like the American League and the National League (in which the Dodgers also played in Brooklyn at that time). Pitching for the Tip-Tops, Bluejacket became the first pitcher in baseball to win a game without throwing a pitch, when, with two outs in the ninth inning against the Pittsburgh Rebels, he picked a man off first to end the game, and was credited with the win. In 1916 he played for the Cincinnati Reds of the National League.

91. Tonkawa is about 37 miles southwest of Chilocco. It is the seat of the federally recognized Tonkawa Tribe of Oklahoma.
92. If Delgadillo's approximate date of birth for Charles Martine Jr., 1886, is correct, and if Kenoi is accurate in describing him here in 1902, then he would already have studied horticulture for six years at Chilocco, worked at a Ute Indian school, and now gained employment as disciplinarian for the older children—all by the time he was no more than (about) sixteen years old! He would, as noted, later go on to the Hampton Institute.

2. Dan Nicholas's School Years

1. An undated, handwritten manuscript in Ball's papers headed, "Chapter/ Dan Nicholas," notes of James Nicholas that he was "one of Victorio's runners. That position was one of great responsibility."
2. Naiche, sometimes written, Natchez, was the second son of Cochise, born about 1857. He became the leader of the Chokonen band of Chiricahua Apaches after the death of his older brother, Taza, and he fought both Mexicans and Americans alongside Geronimo. After the 1886 surrender, he was among those—Geronimo, Loco, Fun, Chappo, Perico—imprisoned at Fort Pickens, 400 miles from Fort Marion, where the women and children were held, and he eventually was sent to Fort Sill. When the Apache prisoners were allowed to leave Oklahoma in 1913, Naiche was among those who went to the Mescalero reservation in the Southwest. He died in 1921.
3. That is, until they were seven or perhaps eight years old, after which they played apart.
4. Delgadillo records Elsie Nicholas's death as April 1901 (Delgadillo 2013, 207), when her son, Dan, would have been seven.

5. Minnie is his younger sister, born in June 1898 (Delgadillo 2013, 208). She would have been only three when her mother died in 1901, and so not yet going to school.
6. This would be about 1901 or 1902, and the "school bus" would still have been a horse-drawn "kids hack," not yet a motorized vehicle.
7. The Dutch Reformed Church's mission school at Fort Sill opened in 1899, run by the church but largely funded by the government.
8. This was likely the Rev. L. L. Legters, first pastor of the Comanche Reformed Church.
9. Robert Gooday was about a year older than Nicholas, according to his Chilocco record, and he attended the school from 1907 to 1913 (okhistory.org/research/chiloccosearch). John Tahnitoe, born in 1895, was the son of John Tahnitoe Sr., a close friend of Naiche's and well known as a medicine person (Delgadillo 2013, 246). I have not identified Nelson.
10. After the death of both his parents, John Allard was adopted by John Allard about 1908, taking his stepfather's name. He attended Chilocco from 1910 to 1913, when he went to Mescalero (Delgadillo 2013, 6). He, too, was an important consultant to Morris Opler in the 1930s.

    When the Apaches arrived at Fort Sill in 1894, Agent Hugh L. Scott had them establish twelve villages, each known by the name of a particular headman, thus, "Geronimo's Village," "Loco's Village," and "Naiche's Village," among others. As noted earlier, Jason Betzinez gave a list of all twelve villages and their locations (Betzinez 1988, 167), as did Harry Mithlo from the account of his father, Watson (Mithlo and Beasley 2020, 128). Watson Mithlo had said that "Naiche's village was the main Apache meeting place" for gambling, dancing, and socializing (128).
11. The rule generally at the boarding schools was English only. But even Richard Pratt at Carlisle allowed the use of Native languages when Indian guests arrived.
12. "Loco was the last chief of the Warm Springs Apaches" (Delgadillo 2013, 160), whose name—Spanish for "crazy"—was meant as praise for daring in battle. His band had surrendered to General Crook in 1883, and some of them served as government scouts during the Geronimo campaign of 1886. They were nonetheless sent as prisoners to Fort Marion, then to Alabama, before being relocated to Fort Sill. Watson Mithlo is reported as saying: "We never forgave the scouts for what they did to us during those terrible days. Bad blood lingers to this day" (Mithlo and Beasley 2020, 30).

13. Four Mile Crossing is where Naiche's village was located, and it is now within the city of Lawton in Comanche County, Oklahoma.
14. Like Sam Kenoi, a great many Native American people played American baseball. Here, by noting that the baseball played was "(Indian)," Nicholas means to say that this was not American baseball, but rather a version of the stick ball game played by many Native nations. A game more like lacrosse than baseball, Indian stick ball would be played by teams on which the number of players varied and could be quite large. Rules also varied, but the object generally was to drive the ball across the goal of the opposing team. The hoop and pole game "was played throughout the entire continent north of Mexico," and was "remarkable for the wide diversity in the form of the implements employed, as well as in the method of play" (Culin 1992, 420). Opler wrote that among the Chiricahua Apaches, "two men slide poles after a hoop; the object is to make the hoop fall upon the butt end of the pole. Pole and hoop are marked with incised bands, and, according to the relationship of these bands after the throw, a count is made. The game has definite ceremonial overtones" (Opler 1941, 49). The rock game was a type of hand game in which one side hid a rock and the other attempted to guess which member of the opposing team had it. All these games involved substantial betting.
15. Eve Ball noted that "Old Nicholas," Dan's father, "had a cousin, Kaydezhinne, who shared the privilege of being a runner," and I suspect this is "old man Katizini," born about 1861. Delgadillo reports that he, too, was a scout for the army during the final Geronimo campaign, and he joined those who went to Mescalero from Fort Sill in 1913 (Delgadillo 2013, 142–43).
16. Sam Binday, born about 1858, was, according to Alicia Delgadillo, "likely the son of the famous Chiricahua shaman She-neah" (Delgadillo 2013, 25). It is not clear why it was thought that any powers he had were being put to malign purposes. Nicholas takes up his visits to Binday later in the narrative.
17. Binday had been married to Effie Zaienah, who had attended Carlisle. She died in 1900 and Binday "never remarried after Effie's death" (Delgadillo 2013, 25).
18. Bessie had been married to Simeon Nashdelten, with whom she had two children: a girl named Ruby, who died in 1900, and a boy named Walter, born in 1902, the year her husband, Simeon, died. Shortly after his death, she married Clement Seanilizay, with whom she would also have two children: Emerson, born in 1904, and George, born in 1908 (Delgadillo 2013, 115). Dan Nicholas has recalled the time he cared for

these children as about 1904, at which time Bessie would have had a boy of two and a newborn baby boy.

19. Grover Kaitah is probably the son of the Chiricahua army scout Kayitah who, with his cousin, Martine, persuaded Geronimo to surrender. But Delgadillo has no entry for a Grover Kayitah. She does list a Gsorn Kayitah—an unusual name—as the son of Martine, who died in 1905. It is not clear what year Nicholas is discussing, but this might be the friend to whom he is referring. Paul Guydelkon Jr. was the same age as Dan Nicholas. He too attended Chilocco (1907–8), and was among those who went to Mescalero in 1913. Clarence is probably Clarence Jolsanny, about the same age as Dan Nicholas, and whose attendance at Chilocco largely coincided with his. I have not identified Mrs. Stevens.
20. Coyote is an Apache trickster, on the one hand, someone with more-than-natural powers but also someone who grossly and bawdily transgresses against cultural norms. Stories about him are set in the earliest times, when the earth was still "soft" and the ways of the people not fully established, although Coyote is still out and about even today. Near the beginning of his autobiographical narrative, Sam Kenoi narrated no fewer than forty-four Coyote stories (Kenoi 193?, ms. 31–112) to Morris Opler, almost surely in English. He had previously told eight Coyote stories to Harry Hoijer in Apache. See Webster (1999) for commentary on these latter.
21. David Fatty, Sam Kenoi's stepfather, was apparently fat, like his own father, Gordo. But he was some twenty-five years younger than Geronimo, who about this time—it is again not clear exactly what year Nicholas is referring to—would have been close to eighty, his age very likely explaining some of what Nicholas calls his absent-mindedness.
22. This is Charles Istee, born about 1872, whom we have encountered earlier and will hear of further. He had been sent in 1887 from Fort Marion to Carlisle, where he remained until 1895, when he was sent back to Fort Sill. He was a farmer and also worked in the government Indian Service at the Comanche Indian School. He was among those who went to Mescalero in 1913 (Delgadillo 2013, 122).
23. Eve Ball's 1968 autobiographical typescript for Nicholas has him remember, "Geronimo was well treated at Fort Sill. He got a checkup every month. He was treated well and got better treatment than the rest."
24. A great many observers have reported Geronimo's entrepreneurial inclinations. The bows he made were for sale, and, although he may not have signed them, he made other things that he did sign, signed items bringing a substantially greater price than unsigned items. Trudy Griffin-

Pierce writes that "Geronimo had ten thousand dollars in the bank when he died" in 1909 (Griffin-Pierce 2006, 70). That would be well over a quarter of a million dollars today (2021).

25. Apache people, like most southwestern Indigenous peoples—as noted earlier—were concerned that the ghosts of the deceased would return and cause trouble if not actual harm; certain illnesses or anxious states were also often believed to be the doing of ghosts. One of Geronimo's powers was the ability to achieve the cure of someone thus troubled. It is also the case that sometimes the cause of sickness or malaise was suspected to be the malign influence of the trickster, Coyote, and Geronimo's "coyote power" enabled him to achieve cures in these instances as well. Watson Mithlo is quoted as affirming that "Geronimo was a medicine man and a warrior," although "never a chief," and stating that "Geronimo's medicine was so strong he could hold back the dawn" (Mithlo and Beasley 2020, 138).
26. "Ndendai" is Opler's spelling here for the Nedhni Apache band to which Geronimo, like the Nedhni chief, Juh, a cousin of Geronimo mentioned earlier, belonged. Asa is Daklugie, Juh's son, born about 1874, and a nephew of Geronimo. Daklugie traveled to Mescalero in 1908 to evaluate it as a possible future home for the Fort Sill Apaches, and he was a strong advocate of the move west in 1913 (Delgadillo 2013, 61). He died in 1955.
27. Captain Hugh L. Scott was the Fort Sill agent in 1894 when the Apaches arrived, but whatever year this was—Nicholas once more does not make the chronology of events clear—the agent was Lieutenant Francis Henry Beech.
28. Arnold Kinzhuna, born in 1866, had attended Carlisle in 1887–89, after service as an army scout, and so might have been a good choice as an interpreter.
29. This would be about 1905, when Samuel Melville Barrett, superintendent of education in Lawton, Oklahoma Territory, obtained permission from President Theodore Roosevelt—in whose inaugural parade Geronimo had ridden—to record an autobiography from Geronimo. Daklugie served as interpreter. Barrett published *Geronimo's Story of His Life* in 1906 (see Geronimo 1973).
30. The cause of the sickness would probably have been some form of improper behavior toward these animals. This and the following three paragraphs appear in edited form in Opler's *Apache Lifeway* (Opler 1941, 40–41).

31. Opler quotes Nicholas on this matter in *Apache Lifeway*, but in the version published there, he gives only the English words. Thus, *Tsa* is "an old black tray basket," *ditcile* is "an abalone shell," and *tadidin* is "a bag of pollen" (Opler 1941, 40).
32. Four is the Apache pattern number, as it is for a great many Native nations. Ceremonies usually take four days, requests will be made four times, and many other ritual or mundane actions have fourfold repetitions.
33. He is referring to the very important Apache girls' puberty ceremony, for which a ceremonial tepee is erected. Opler observed: "This is a ceremony at which all members of the tribe feel welcome" (1941, 91). As noted, Nicholas published an ethnographic paper on the Mescalero girls' puberty ceremony in 1939, while as early as perhaps 1898–99, Naiche had done hide paintings of the Chiricahua girls' puberty ceremony. For Naiche, see Griffin-Pierce (2006). Harry Hoijer published a number of song texts from the ceremony that Dr. Jules Henry had heard sung by David Fatty, and in his notes to Hoijer's publication, Morris Opler provided a substantial commentary on one of them (Hoijer 1938, 149–53).
34. Opler included an edited version of this paragraph in *Apache Lifeway* (Opler 1941, 43). He notes there: "Sometimes the child's panic reaches such proportions that a ceremony must be conducted over him" (43). We will see further that although Nicholas's fear of ghosts is very great, he describes no such ceremony being performed for him. Geronimo, as Nicholas said, was someone with "ghost power," so had he been asked, he might have conducted the necessary ceremony for Dan Nicholas.
35. Nicholas would have been about fourteen in 1908, and the "trouble" referred to seems to have been at Fort Sill. But 1908 was his second year at the Chilocco Indian School, so this incident must have occurred at some point when he had returned to Fort Sill from school. The school the Comanche girl informs of her being assaulted, in the next paragraph, is the mission school that Nicholas himself had formerly attended.
36. Kenoi had spoken of Martine, known as Charles Martine, who, along with Kaitah, had tracked Geronimo and persuaded him to surrender, both of them being sent to Fort Marion as prisoners nonetheless. He, too, went to Mescalero in 1913, where he died in 1937. I do not know exactly what he had told Opler about these matters.
37. The Sunday School movement was independent of the religious services of any given Christian denomination, and, for the most part, in the United States, involved the study of selected Bible passages.

38. Old Man Cooney is William Coonie, born about 1865. He was another of the Apaches who, despite having served as a government scout, was imprisoned in Florida and Alabama before being sent to Fort Sill. Sam Haozous, born in 1868, was Nicholas's cousin, related to Regis Alchintoyah (Delgadillo 2013, 113), and so possibly to Sam Kenoi as well. Like Nicholas, he was an army bugler (Skinner 1987, 355). Sam Haozous's son with his last wife, Blossom White, was the celebrated artist Allen Houser (1914–94); their grandson, Michael Darrow, is currently the tribal historian for the Fort Sill Apache Tribe.

Upon his arrival at Carlisle in 1887, Jason Betzinez was listed as nineteen, thus with a birthdate of 1868. But when he came to Fort Sill in 1900, he reported that interpreter George Wratten "gave the date of 1860 as [his] birthdate" (Delgadillo 2013, 20). He thus chose to celebrate "his one hundredth birthday at Fort Sill in the company of more than one hundred friends and officers of the post" on the fourth of July—a date he had chosen himself for his birthday—of 1960, just four months before his death (Delgadillo 2013, 21). A blacksmith and farmer, Betzinez remained in Oklahoma rather than relocating to Mescalero, and in 1919 married the field matron and missionary, Anna Heersma, whom he had first met in 1907 (Betzinez 1988, 203, 205). Watson Mithlo also decided upon a July 4, 1886, birthday, as noted earlier, although an April date and other years have been given as well. Harry Mithlo represents his father as saying of Betzinez—the first part contrary to what others have reported—that "he was a ferocious warrior when he was young, but when he got older he became a kind of fuddy-duddy" (75), reporting to the Fort Sill authorities instances of Apache drinking, gambling, and engaging in traditional dances; he disapproved of all these.

Carlos Keanie, according to his Chilocco record—in the Chilocco Index he is called Keamie—was born about 1888, and attended the school in 1905–8. He, too, went to Mescalero in 1913, but returned to Oklahoma the following year. "He married Martha Prince, a Dutch Reformed Missionary," and died in 1923 (Delgadillo 2013, 149). I have not found a James Koakly, although the Chilocco Index does record a James Holly, an Apache from Fort Sill, as having attended the school for a year in 1902–3.

39. This was Ruth Keanie.

40. Eugene Chihuahua (1879–1965) was the son of Chihuahua, a prominent leader who headed his own village at Fort Sill. Eugene took over as village head upon his father's death in 1901. As noted earlier, he had not

gone to Carlisle as had his sister, Ramona, who married Daklugie. With Daklugie, he actively supported the move to Mescalero.

41. Tooisgah, listed on his Carlisle application form in 1911 at a little over 5'9," was surely bigger than Dan Nicholas, who had said that he was slightly built. He spent 1907–8 at the Chilocco Indian School—its Index gives his age in 1908 as fifteen, which, if correct, would make him only a year older than Nicholas—before enrolling at Carlisle in 1911, and leaving in 1914. He remained in Oklahoma and took an allotment (Delgadillo 2013, 258). In 1916 he wrote to Carlisle superintendent Oscar Lipps to say that he was "glad to get the Arrow"—one of the Carlisle newspapers—"for the opening of the school year of 1916"; that he was "still farming a little," and that he missed "Carlisle a whole lot."
42. Apaches had not traditionally eaten fish, so perhaps that is why John Tooisgah gets angry when he is called "fisherman." But his generation seems to have learned to like fish well enough. Jason Betzinez recalled as "One of [his] most pleasant memories . . . eating oysters at a little stand back of the market square" in Carlisle, Pennsylvania, while making the point that this was "a bit unusual for a western Indian, whose tribe had a taboo against eating anything that lived under water" (Betzinez 1988, 155). Based on accounts in Eve Ball's papers, Sherry Robinson wrote that Sam "Kenoi was one of the few Apaches to enjoy fishing and eating fish" (Robinson 2000, 106). As Nicholas goes on to make clear, Tooisgah shared his fish with other Apache students—all of whom seemed happy enough to eat what "lived under water."
43. This is John Tahnitoe Sr., born about 1855. He was a close friend of Naiche and a noted medicine person. He had also served as a government scout (Delgadillo 2013, 246). The time would have been about 1900.
44. This is Sam Binday's son, Vincent, born in 1893, and so a year older than Dan Nicholas. He lived only until 1909. His older brother, Hobson, died the following year at the age of nineteen. The boys' sister, Fannie, had died as a child of four in 1896 (Delgadillo 2013, 26), so that whatever powers their father, Sam, might have had, he could not protect his children from harm.
45. This is Watson Mithlo, Laurence Mithlo's son, who, whether born in 1886, 1888, 1892, or 1893, is still older than Dan Nicholas. He did not go to Mescalero but remained in Oklahoma, where many Mithlos currently reside.
46. This is the first of only three places in the manuscript where Opler's notation, "(laughter)," indicates that he is transcribing an oral narration. This is to say that it tells the reader either that Dan Nicholas laughed as

he told this to Opler, and/or that there were others present—as was traditional with oral narrative—who laughed. Nicholas and any audience he had besides Opler may, of course, have laughed at other points in the story—or paused, frowned, or registered other emotions: but Opler—perhaps after some deliberation—did not choose to report them except on this and one other occasion, on p. 72.

47. Nicholas calls Watson Mithlo "Watson Mailo," as we have seen. In Nicholas's Chiricahua Apache speech "maitso/maicho" is the word for "wolf or large coyote," or, as Nicholas teases here, "fox." Professor Anthony Webster kindly provided the linguistic information (pers. comm., December 12, 2021).

48. Don Tooisgah, John's brother, born in 1896, was "named Albert . . . but was called Don," for reasons I have not discovered. Although he had attended school from 1902 to 1912, he was placed in the third grade when he entered Chilocco in 1912. He there contracted tuberculosis, for which school officials wished to send him to Phoenix in the hope that the climate would be beneficial. His parents, however, did not wish him to go. He returned home, where he died in 1913 (Delgadillo 2013, 23).

49. Hugh Coonie was the son of William Coonie, whom Nicholas had called "Old Man Coony." His Chilocco record has him as Hugh Connie, and he attended from 1908 to 1911. The boys treat Don Tooisgah as a "baby," although, according to Alicia Delgadillo, he was born in 1893, and thus would actually be a year older than Nicholas (Delgadillo 2013, 58).

50. At this point Nicholas is boarding at the school, with—as he has described it so far—only Saturday free to visit his relatives. I assume he means that sometimes when his father visited, he left school with him and went to his home, instead of going to his aunt Bessie.

51. In *Indeh*, Eve Ball called Dan Nicholas "one of the best educated and most intellectual members of his tribe" (Ball et al. 1988, 59). She cites him as having said of Apache religion that it "emphasized the life on earth through rites and ceremonies. . . . Nothing was ever said of reward or punishment. They emphasized good behavior. . . . It was not a matter of future punishment, but of doing right because it was right" (59).

52. Yeye seems to be Nicholas's name for the Apache Giver of Life who is usually called Yusn, Usen, or Ussen, a name that may echo Jesus. Nicholas later discusses the Giver of Life further and offers many thoughts on the differences between Apache traditional religion and Christianity.

53. This is the Reverend Frank Hall Wright (1860–1922), part Choctaw and known as the "Indian Evangelist." Supported by the Dutch Reformed Church, he first preached at Fort Sill about 1898.

54. Carlos Montezuma (1865/6–1923), a Yavapai, had been captured by Tohon'o Akimel (formerly Pima) people when he was about five, and then sold to Carlo Gentile, an Italian photographer and prospector, who gave him his name and raised him. For these reasons, he had had only little experience of his people's traditional lifeways. One of the first Native American medical doctors, Montezuma received his degree from the Chicago Medical College in 1889. As we have seen, he was visited at his practice in Chicago by Sam Kenoi.
55. Pressure to give up Indian beliefs and accept Christian doctrine exclusively would have come mostly from the missionaries. At least some Apache Christians, as Nicholas notes, were comfortable integrating Apache and Christian beliefs or adhering to them in parallel fashion.
56. Silas John Edwards was a Western Apache born about the mid-1880s in Arizona Territory. After a visionary experience, he preached a religion that mingled traditional Apache beliefs and practices with Christianity, to which he added elements from the Hopi Snake Dance. About 1904 he developed a symbolic writing system to promulgate his beliefs. In 1933, about the time Nicholas narrated, John's wife was brutally murdered, a crime for which he was—perhaps wrongfully—convicted, leading to his spending twenty years in prison.
57. This would be the sort of ghost sickness that Geronimo was supposed to have power to treat, although Dan Nicholas did not undergo one of his curing ceremonies.
58. As noted earlier and apparent here, Apaches avoid speaking the names of the dead.
59. Many Native people were afraid of the American hospitals for the simple reason that many had died in them. Anxiety about ghosts was general throughout Apache culture although obviously some were more concerned than others; Dan Nicholas was, and Sam Kenoi was not. It is quite possible that Nicholas Sr. and Naiche are carrying on their conversation expressly to tease Dan Nicholas.
60. Ben Astoyeh was born about 1862. He had more than once served as a government scout, and he had also developed a bad reputation for drinking. Whoever may have died in the house he had occupied, he lived until 1934.
61. The deity Nicholas refers to as Changing Woman—an important Navajo deity—is more usually called White Painted Woman by Apaches. White Painted Woman had two sons, Child of Water, the Apache culture hero, and his brother, Enemy Slayer or Killer of Enemies.

62. Opler quotes this from Nicholas—without identifying him—to conclude a section on gift-giving in *An Apache Lifeway* (Opler 1941, 400). He also printed a slightly different version of what Nicholas says on the previous page of that book (399), where he glossed it by saying, "Acceptance of a gift is felt by the receiver as a claim upon him to be adjusted in his own time and way" (399).
63. Opler published a different version of this in *Apache Lifeway*. There, Hugh Chee, a nephew of Cochise, born about 1872, who attended Carlisle in 1886–96, is identified only as "C." (Opler 1941, 399), and in an observation that is not strictly in accord with Nicholas's statement, Opler writes that "these gifts set up currents of reciprocity which stimulate the exchange and circulation of property" (400), the usual anthropological understanding of tribal gift-giving.
64. An Apache dietary taboo. Apaches also did not traditionally eat pork—something they were regularly served while imprisoned at Fort Marion. Watson Mithlo affirmed that it was "taboo for an Apache to eat or kill a pig" (Mithlo and Beasley 2020, 81).
65. Born about 1854, Chatto raided both Americans and Mexicans—who captured his second wife and two children in 1883. He joined the U.S. army's scouts in the hope of gaining his family's return, but was unsuccessful. He had a generally untrustworthy reputation among his fellow Apaches, and before Geronimo left San Carlos in 1885, such was the enmity between him and Chatto that Geronimo apparently ordered him killed. Chatto was not killed, however, but served in the campaign against Geronimo, which service did not prevent his being sent to Fort Marion and then to Alabama as a prisoner of war (Delgadillo 2013, 35). Later, at Fort Sill, he had his own village, along with Martine, Loco, and his old nemesis, Geronimo. In 1913 he went to Mescalero, where he died in 1934 (Delgadillo 2013, 37).
66. Again, this is the Apache girls' puberty ceremony. The "expense" of the ceremony was borne by the family of the girl, with—since it was indeed expensive—others in the community contributing. It is quite certain that the American "agent and missionaries" disapproved of the ceremony for reasons other than its "expense."
67. This is Sam Kenoi, almost twenty years older than Nicholas, who, by the time Dan Nicholas narrated at Mescalero, was, as noted, usually called Sam Chino.
68. *Tiswin* is a mild beer made from maize, and the only alcoholic beverage "which is made or consumed in appreciable quantities" (Opler 1941, 368) by Apaches traditionally. But there is some confusion here: if Nicholas

is about fourteen at this time, his grandmother had died some years ago. Naiche's first wife had been Nahdeyole, whom he had divorced about 1892–93; she had died in 1896 (Delgadillo 2013, 185). At this time, Naiche had two wives: Ecclaheh (75) and Haozinhe (112). Nicholas does not say which of them had extended the invitation to the drinking party.

69. As noted earlier, here and soon following are the second and third—and the last—times Opler recorded a response to the narration by Nicholas and/or others.
70. This is Espida or Erick Spitty, born about 1868 (Delgadillo 2013, 236). Opler observed: "The preparation of beverages, both alcoholic and nonalcoholic, is classified with cooking and is, therefore, the task of the woman" (Opler 1941, 368). He then paraphrased Nicholas's remark here, withholding the name of Nicholas's uncle: "One man used to make it, but he was a roughneck, and didn't care about his standing. He lowered himself many times" (368). Opler did not, as elsewhere in *An Apache Lifeway*, identify the consultant he was quoting.
71. Opler noted that "children are directed to make a respectful spitting noise when the lightning flashes and to refrain from eating during a storm" (1941, 38). Lightning, associated with the Thunder People, can be harmful in other ways than by striking someone. Opler writes: "Sage is a most generally used prophylactic against lightning sickness. . . . Cudweed is another plant for which similar properties are claimed" (1941, 282). Cudweed or cotton weed can be eaten or used as an herb. In the absence of sage or cudweed, it seems that a bit of grass might be adequate.
72. As stated in note 15, "Simmons," Bessie's first husband, was Simeon Nashdelten, and her second husband, "Clemens," was Clement Seanalizay.
73. If Nicholas is seventeen, the year would be 1911, and that is the year he came back to Fort Sill from Chilocco—which he has not spoken of at all.
74. Chilocco records have Nicholas enrolled from 1907 to 1911. Hugh Connie attended from 1908 to 1911. John Tonitu was enrolled as John Tahinto, and attended in 1907–10, while John Allard was at the school in 1910–13. Seven years older than Dan Nicholas, Harry Perico, son of Perico, went to Chilocco in 1907 and graduated in 1918.
75. A half-day of vocational or agricultural work along with a half-day of class was the regimen at all the government off-reservation boarding schools. Part of Chilocco's "strictness," unmentioned by Nicholas, is that like the other government boarding schools, it was run on a military model, with both male and female students engaging in a good deal of marching and drilling.

76. If the Chilocco records are correct, Nicholas returned to Fort Sill from Chilocco in 1911, but the Apaches did not leave Fort Sill for Mescalero until 1913, two years after he got back.
77. This is Talbot Gooday, Robert's father, born about 1863, twenty-some years older than Bessie, and a former Carlisle student. He and Bessie were married in 1914 (Delgadillo 2013, 102–3).
78. This is Major George W. Goode, the last agent for the Apaches, who served at Fort Sill until 1913. Jason Betzinez speaks of him, on the one hand, favorably as seeking to curtail drinking, gambling, and dancing at Fort Sill, but, on the other hand, unfavorably in that Goode supported the move to Mescalero, something Betzinez opposed (Betzinez 1988, 183–84).
79. Sam Kenoi had told Opler that Major Goode "was no good" (Kenoi 193?, ms. 334), although it is certainly not difficult to understand why the major would be upset with Dan Nicholas on this occasion. As Nicholas says, many Apaches voluntarily chose to attend Haskell, so the only reason sending him there might be punitive is the fact that Nicholas had just recently returned from Chilocco and would not wish to be sent away to school again so soon.
80. This paragraph and the two preceding paragraphs are cited by Opler in *Apache Lifeway* (1941, 148–49) as illustrative of Apache belief "that impregnation cannot occur as a result of a single sexual contact" (148).
81. Minnie Nicholas married a Kiowa Apache man named Zurega and settled in Oklahoma (Delgadillo 2013, 208).

3. VINCENT NATALISH

1. Wratten had gone with the Apaches from Arizona Territory to Florida in 1886, and from there to Mount Vernon Barracks in the spring of 1887, when he married an Apache woman. He and his family then accompanied the Apaches to Fort Sill. Dan Nicholas told Eve Ball he had heard that Wratten started out a harsh man and mistreated the People in Florida and Oklahoma. For some reason he changed his ways and was a real friend to the Chiricahua. He was a sort of general manager for farm and cattle work and a good manager. He was also a good cowboy.
2. All of this and the materials I cite in following paragraphs may be found in the "Documents" section of the Carlisle Digital Resource Center, https://carlisleindian.dickinson.edu/documents, under the heading "Correspondence Regarding Apaches."
3. But if Istee was indeed Victorio's son, he would have been Natalish's uncle.

4. Like some other Carlisle "deserters," however, he would nonetheless communicate with the school years later, filling out and returning a questionnaire he had been sent in 1912.
5. The 1891 graduation had indeed been planned for spring—for May 1—although a measles outbreak at the school caused it to be postponed. But the following year, in 1892, although there were still a few cases of measles, graduation exercises were held early, on February 28, which seems to have marked a shift for several years. I thank Jim Gerencser of the Carlisle Indian School Project for much of this information (pers. comm., September 15, 2021).
6. As we shall see later, Carlisle's last superintendent, John Francis, invited Vincent Natalish to visit the school during the 1918 exercises, to be held in June. The school closed permanently that September.
7. The March 1899 issue of the Carlisle *Red Man* is not on the Carlisle School's digital website because, as I learned from Jim Gerencser who runs the site, no original copy of the paper was available for scanning by the Cumberland County Historical Society. It did show up on some scanned microfilm, however, and I am very grateful to Mr. Gerencser for finding it and forwarding it to me.
8. Arizona and New Mexico both became states in 1912, so when Natalish spoke in 1899, they were still Arizona Territory and New Mexico Territory. Natalish was a Warm Springs Apache, from Ojo Caliente—Warm Springs—mostly in New Mexico Territory.
9. This is not quite accurate. Apaches did hunt and gather wild plants, and they also to some extent planted maize, beans, and pumpkins. But an important aspect of Apaches' traditional subsistence was raiding, which Morris Opler, in *An Apache Lifeway*, discussed as an element of "the maintenance of the household" (Opler 19941, x). Miriam Perrett affirms this, adding that raiding was also ceremonial in nature, representing, for young Apache men, "a rite of passage into manhood" (xxiv). The fact of Apache raiding should be noted in relation to Natalish's comment soon to follow that Apaches were considered a "peaceable people."
10. By "Southern Apaches" he may once more be referencing his Warm Springs people. Pinery Canyon is in the Coronado National Forest of southeastern Arizona that also runs into southwestern New Mexico.
11. He may be referring to Tohon'o Akimel (Pima) or Maricopa people.
12. To state the obvious, what Natalish calls the "protection" of the United States might, instead, be called the domination of the United States. And, almost as obvious, conditions varied widely at the many reservations throughout the country.

13. Colonel Bernard Irwin was an assistant army surgeon active among the Apaches in the 1860s, and Dr. Walter Reed, who discovered and/or confirmed the cause of yellow fever, had served among them in the Southwest in the 1870s. But I have found nothing to suggest that either of these doctors would have known the tribes of the Pacific coast—whose environments and cultures differed greatly from those of the Apaches.
14. The phrase calling Apaches "the tiger of the human species" is generally attributed to General George Crook, who was, in charge of the Geronimo campaign just before its end.
15. Cody, a pony express rider, a soldier for the Union Army, and a scout for the government in the Indian wars, had already published an autobiography twenty years earlier, in 1879, even before he had staged and begun to tour with his Buffalo Bill's Wild West in 1883. His sister, Helen Cody Wetmore, had only that year, 1899, published *Last of the Great Scouts: The Life Story of William F. Cody, "Buffalo Bill,"* and the book may have come to Natalish's attention.
16. He may indeed remember this: but he was then a boy of about seven.
17. As his audience might or might not have understood, this refers to the fact that Natalish would take an allotment of land at Fort Sill, which meant that under the provisions of the 1887 Dawes Act he would in time acquire U.S. citizenship.
18. The first Native American to graduate from Yale was Henry Roe Cloud, a Winnebago, and a member of the class of 1910. As we will see further, Natalish and Roe Cloud almost surely knew one another, although not through any common association with Yale.
19. Larré seems to have taken this as well from the *Times*. A brief notice of Natalish in a piece in the *Times* for December 15, 1912, and headlined "Indians Do Well in City," reported that Natalish had "studied engineering at Carlisle" (Larré 2012, 80).
20. But the piece in the *Eagle* contained errors, reporting, for example, that Natalish had left Carlisle "about two years ago," although he had, in fact, graduated in 1899, thirteen years earlier.
21. He would go on to become vice president under Herbert Hoover, from 1928 to 1932, the first person of color to serve as vice president of the United States before Kamala Harris. He and Hoover would lose in a landslide to Franklin D. Roosevelt and John Nance Garner in the election of 1932.
22. He was the grandson of the warrior Chatto, who had ridden with Cochise. He later served as one of General Crook's army scouts in the Geronimo campaign, but was nonetheless sent to Florida as a prisoner of war. He would go to Mescalero in 1913.

23. By this time Henry Roe Cloud had also become involved in the negotiations regarding the Fort Sill Apaches on the basis of his association, dating from around 1910, with the Reverend Walter Roe and his wife Mary—Cloud would take their name as his middle name. The Roes had a mission at Colony, Oklahoma, not far from Fort Sill, and had been concerned with the Apache situation. In 1917 the Cherokee writer, John Milton Oskison observed that Natalish and Roe Cloud "very largely organized and directed the fight made on behalf of that band of prisoner Apaches to be given allotments of land in Oklahoma" (in Larré 2012, 454). This is something of an exaggeration, although it testifies to a relation between the two men that has otherwise been ignored. COVID has prevented me from going through the Roe Cloud Papers at Yale, and an online search has not turned up any correspondence between them, although I suspect the two probably did exchange letters.
24. Globe is just off the San Carlos reservation—the boundaries of which were altered after silver was discovered in the 1870s to prevent the Apaches from having any claims to it. Miami, also close to the reservation, and about 6 miles west of Globe, was incorporated in 1909, after copper was discovered there. Copper mining began in Miami in 1911 and continues to this day (2021). The other places Natalish mentions are all small towns in Gila County, Arizona. I provide notes for any information about them I have found.
25. There are two Wheatfields in Arizona, one in Apache County on the border with New Mexico that is part of the Navajo Nation, and the one referenced here, in Gila County, about 10 miles northwest of Globe. After the 1848 discovery of gold in California, a large number of Chinese emigrated to the state, where they suffered violent discrimination. Upon the passage of aggressively anti-Chinese legislation in the 1870s, many moved to Arizona, where some found work on the construction of the Southern Pacific Railroad. They suffered further state and local discrimination after the passage of the federal Chinese Exclusion Act of 1882, but at the state and territorial level this appears to have been somewhat less virulent in Arizona than in California. Although a number of Chinese people moved to Arizona's larger cities, where they operated restaurants, grocery stores, and laundries, a number of them acquired sufficient land to farm. The "white community" was generally hostile to both Chinese and Indians. See Pugsley (2003).
26. "Mr. Packard" is Florance Amynander Packard (1850–1932), who seems to have owned not only "most of the valley" but also a grocery store in

town. He was noted for the many mountain lions he hunted and killed, both because the lions were a danger to his livestock and for sport.

27. These had, generally, been Crook's promises to the Apache scouts. But Crook at the end of the Geronimo campaign, was replaced by General Nelson Miles, who did not consider himself bound by promises Crook had made, and who sent the scouts as prisoners of war to Florida along with Geronimo's rebels. Crook actively sought the redress of this injustice for years.
28. Born on the Seneca reservation in New York in 1881, Parker was an archeologist, a historian, and an activist for Indian rights. He was among the founders of the Society of American Indians in 1911, and in 1915–20 served as editor of its *American Indian Magazine*. Many years later, he directed President Franklin Roosevelt's Works Progress Administration's Indian Arts Project. He died in 1955.
29. John Milton Oskison (1874–1947) was born in Indian Territory to an English father and part-Cherokee mother. He attended Stanford University and was its first Native American graduate in 1898. He briefly attended graduate school at Harvard, leaving to devote himself to writing fiction. He was a featured speaker at Carlisle's 1912 commencement exercises, and he addressed the Carlisle student body on other occasions. Oskison served in World War I and worked as a journalist, historian, and activist for Native rights. See Larré 2012.
30. Fort Sill would again hold innocent people as prisoners when it served as a camp for interned Japanese-Americans in 1942, during the Second World War. As of June 2019, it held Mexican and Central American immigrant children of varying status.
31. For an account of the 1914 congressional hearings, see chapter 4 of my *Boarding School Voices* (Krupat 2021).
32. Jacksonville is about 40 miles north-northwest of Saint Augustine, where the Apache prisoners of war had been held in 1886–87, and it is possible that even so many years later its citizens maintained an interest in the fate of those Apaches.
33. The letter may be found in Vincent Natalish's Carlisle student file.
34. In 1917 John Oskison had written that Natalish held "a place in the Bureau of Highways of New York City" (in Larré 2012, 454), continuing, it would seem, to work in civil engineering.
35. Francis's letter may also be found in Vincent Natalish's Carlisle student file.

References

Adams, David Wallace. 1995. *Education for Extinction: American Indians and the Boarding School Experience, 1875–1928*. Lawrence: University Press of Kansas.

Anderson, Robert Jr. 2020. Personal communication, July 24, 2020.

Apess, William. 1992 [1831]. "A Son of the Forest." In Barry O'Connell, ed., *On Our Own Ground: The Complete Writings of William Apess, a Pequot*, 1–97. Amherst: University of Massachusetts Press.

Bahr, Diana Meyers. 2014. *The Students of Sherman Indian School*. Norman: University of Oklahoma Press.

Ball, Eve, compiler, 197?. "Oral History Dan Nicholas." Eve Ball Papers, L. Tom Perry Special Collections, Brigham Young University, box 7, folder 13.

———. 197?a. "Oral History of Sam Kenoi." Eve Ball Papers, L. Tom Perry Special Collections, Brigham Young University, box 6, folder 3.

Ball, Eve, with Nora Henn and Lynda Sanchez. 1988 [1980]. *Indeh: An Apache Odyssey*. Norman: University of Oklahoma Press.

Bell, Genevieve. 1998. "Telling Stories out of School: Remembering the Carlisle Indian Industrial School, 1879–1918." PhD diss., Stanford University.

Bennett, Kay. 1964. *Kaibah: Recollection of a Navajo Girlhood*. Los Angeles: Westernlore.

Berry, Brewton. 1968. *The Education of the American Indian: A Survey of the Literature*. Washington DC: U.S. Department of Health, Education, and Welfare Bureau of Research.

Betzinez, Jason, with Wilbur S. Nye. 1988 [1959]. *I Fought with Geronimo*. Lincoln: University of Nebraska Press.

Bighorse, Tiana. 1990. *Bighorse the Warrior*. Ed. Noel Bennett. Tucson: University of Arizona Press.

Boyer, Ruth. 1992. *Apache Mothers and Daughters: Four Generations of a Family*. Norman: University of Oklahoma Press.

Brown, Estelle. 1952. *Stubborn Fool: A Narrative*. Caldwell ID: Caxton.
Brudvig, Jon. 1994. "Hampton Institute–American Indian Students, 1878–1923. Male students: names G to O." www.twofrog.com/hamptonmale2.txt.
———. 1996. "Bridging the Cultural Divide: American Indians at Hampton Institute, 1878–1923." PhD diss., College of William and Mary.
Brumble, H. David. 1981. *An Annotated Bibliography of American Indian and Eskimo Autobiographies*. Lincoln: University of Nebraska Press.
Brumley, Kim. 2010. *Chilocco: Memories of a Native American Boarding School*. Fairfax OK: Guardian Publishing.
Buchowska, Suzanna. 2016. *Negotiating Native American Identities: The Role of Tradition, Narrative, and Language at Haskell Indian Nations University*. Poznan, Poland: UAM.
Child, Brenda. 1998. *Boarding School Seasons: American Indian Families, 1900–1940*. Lincoln: University of Nebraska Press.
Chilocco Indian School Index. [1884–1980]. Oklahoma Historical Society, okhistory.org/research/chiloccosearch.
Chino, Mark. 2021. Personal communication, July 28, 2021.
Cobb, Amanda. 2000. *Listening to Our Grandmothers' Stories: The Bloomfield Academy for Chickasaw Females, 1852–1949*. Lincoln: University of Nebraska Press.
Coleman, Michael. 1993. *American Indian Children at School, 1850–1930*. Jackson: University Press of Mississippi.
Culin, Stewart. 1992 [1907]. *Games of the North American Indians*. Lincoln: University of Nebraska Press.
Darrow, Michael. 2021. Personal communication, July 28, 2021.
Delgadillo, Alicia. 2013. *From Fort Marion to Fort Sill*. Lincoln: University of Nebraska Press.
Dyk, Walter. 1964 [1947]. *Old Mexican: A Navaho Autobiography*. New York: Johnson.
———. 1967 [1938]. *Son of Old Man Hat: A Navaho Autobiography*. Lincoln: University of Nebraska Press.
Dyk, Walter, and Ruth Dyk. 1980. *Left Handed: A Navajo Autobiography*. New York: Columbia University Press.
Ellis, Clyde. 1996. *To Change Them Forever: Indian Education at the Rainy Mountain Boarding School, 1893–1926*. Norman: University of Oklahoma Press.
Emery, Jacqueline. 2017. *Recovering Native American Writing in the Boarding School Press*. Lincoln: University of Nebraska Press.

Farrer, Claire. 1992. "Living Names and Dead Traditions: Commentary on *Indeh* Review by Dunaway." *Journal of American Folklore* 105: 342–43.

Fear-Segal, Jacqueline. 2007. *White Man's Club: Schools, Race, and the Struggle of Indian Acculturation*. Lincoln: University of Nebraska Press.

Fear-Segal, Jacqueline, and Barbara Rose, eds. 2016. *Carlisle Indian Industrial School: Indigenous Histories, Memories, and Reclamations*. Lincoln: University of Nebraska Press.

Gerencser, Jim. 2021. Personal communication, September 15, 2021.

Geronimo. *Geronimo's Story of His Life*. 1973 [1906]. Ed. S. M. Barrett. Williamstown MA: Cornerhouse.

Gilbert, Matthew Sakiestewa. 2010. *Education Beyond the Mesas: Hopi Students at Sherman Institute, 1902–1929*. Lincoln: University of Nebraska Press.

Gram, John. 2015. *Education at the Edge of Empire: Negotiating Pueblo Identity in New Mexico's Indian Boarding Schools*. Seattle: University of Washington Press.

Greenfeld, Philip. 2001. "Escape from Albuquerque: An Apache Memorate." *American Indian Culture and Research Journal* 25: 47–71.

Griffen, Joyce, ed. 1992. *Lucky the Navajo Singer*, recorded by Alexander and Dorothea Leighton. Albuquerque: University of New Mexico Press.

Griffin-Pierce, Trudy. 2006. *Chiricahua Apache Enduring Power: Naiche's Puberty Ceremony Paintings*. Tuscaloosa: University of Alabama Press.

Haes, Brenda. 1997. "The Incarceration of the Chiricahua Apaches, 1886–1914: A Portrait of Survival." Master of Arts thesis, Texas Tech University.

Hittman, Michael. 1997. *Wovoka and the Ghost Dance*, expanded edition, ed. Don Lynch. Lincoln: University of Nebraska Press.

Hoijer, Harry. 1938. *Chiricahua and Mescalero Apache Texts*, with ethnological notes by Morris Edward Opler. Chicago: University of Chicago Press.

Hyer, Sally. 1990. *One House, One Voice, One Heart: Native American Education at the Santa Fe Indian School*. Santa Fe: Museum of New Mexico Press.

The Indian's Friend. 1903. December.

The Indian Helper. 1891. January 30, 1891.

Indian School Journal. 1906. November.

Indian School Journal. 1909. November.

Johnson, Broderick, ed. 1977. *Stories of Traditional Navajo Life and Culture: Alk'idaa' Yeek'ehgo Dine Keedahat'inee Baa Nahane', by Twenty-Two Navajo Men and Women*. Tsaile, Navajo Nation AZ: *Navajo Community College Press*.

Kabotie, Fred. 1977. *Fred Kabotie: Hopi Indian Artist. An Autobiography told with Bill Belknap*. Flagstaff: Museum of Northern Arizona–Northland.

Katanski, Amelia. 2006. *Learning to Write "Indian": The Boarding School Experience and American Indian Literature*. Norman: University of Oklahoma Press.

Kaywaykla, James. 1970. *In the Days of Victorio: Recollections of a Warm Springs Apache*, ed. Eve Ball. Tucson: University of Arizona Press.

Kenoi, Samuel. 193? "Autobiography of a Chiricahua (Sam Kenoi)," ed. Morris Opler. Morris Opler Papers, #14-25-3238, box 36, folders 2–6, 704 pages. Division of Rare and Manuscript Collections, Karl A. Kroch Library, Cornell University, Ithaca NY.

Kluckhohn, Clyde. 1945. "The Personal Document in Anthropological Science." In Louis Gottschalk, Clyde Kluckhohn, and Robert Angell, *The Use of Personal Documents in History, Anthropology, and Sociology. Social Science Research Council, Bulletin* 53: 77–173.

Krupat, Arnold. 1985. "The Case of Crashing Thunder." In *For Those Who Come After: A Study of Native American Autobiography*, 75–106. Berkeley: University of California Press.

———. 1999. "Foreword" to *Crashing Thunder: The Autobiography of an American Indian*, ed. Paul Radin, ix–xviii. Ann Arbor: University of Michigan Press.

———. 2002. "America's Histories." In *Red Matters: Native American Studies*, 48–75. Philadelphia: University of Pennsylvania Press.

———. 2018. *Changed Forever: American Indian Boarding-School Literature*. Vol. 1. Albany: State University of New York Press.

———. 2020. *Changed Forever: American Indian Boarding-School Literature*. Vol. 2. Albany: State University of New York Press.

———. 2021. *Boarding School Voices: Carlisle Indian Students Speak*. Lincoln: University of Nebraska Press.

L. Tom Perry Special Collections Librarians. Personal communication, September 25, 2021.

LaBarre, Weston. 1989 [1938]. *The Peyote Cult*. Norman: University of Oklahoma Press.

LaFlesche, Francis. 1978 [1900]. *The Middle Five: Indian Schoolboys of the Omaha Tribe*. Lincoln: University of Nebraska Press.

Larré, Lionel, ed. 2012. *Tales of the Old Indian Territory and Essays on the Indian Condition by John Milton Oskison*. Lincoln: University of Nebraska Press.

LaVere, David. 1998. *Life Among the Texas Indians: The WPA Narratives*. College Station: Texas A&M University Press.

Leap, William. 1993. *American Indian English*. Salt Lake City: University of Utah Press.

Lee, George P. 1987. *Silent Courage, an Indian Story: The Autobiography of George P. Lee, a Navajo*. Salt Lake City UT: Deseret.

Lesser, Alexander. 1969 [1933]. *The Pawnee Ghost Dance Hand Game: A Study of Cultural Change*. New York: AMS.

Lindsey, Donal. 1995. *Indians at Hampton Institute, 1877–1923*. Urbana: University of Illinois Press.

Lomawaima, K. Tsianina. 1994. *They Called It Prairie Light: The Story of Chilocco Indian School*. Lincoln: University of Nebraska Press.

Mattina, Anthony. 1985. *The Golden Woman: The Colville Narrative of Peter J. Seymour*. Tucson: University of Arizona Press.

McBeth, Sally. 1983. *Ethnic Identity and the Boarding School Experience of West-Central Oklahoma American Indians*. Lanham MD: University Press of America.

Meriam, Lewis, Ray A. Brown, Henry Roe Cloud, Edward Everett Dale, Emma Duke, Herbert R. Edwards, Fayette Avery McKenzie, Mary Louise Mark, W. Carson Ryan Jr., and William J. Spillman. 1928. *The Problem of Indian Administration: Report of a Survey Made at the Request of the Honorable Hubert Work, Secretary of the Interior, and Submitted to Him, February 21, 1928*. Baltimore: Johns Hopkins University Press.

Mihesuah, Devon. 1993. *Cultivating the Rosebuds: The Education of Women at the Cherokee Female Seminary, 1851–1909*. Urbana: University of Illinois Press.

Mitchell, Frank. 2003 [1978]. *Navaho Blessingway Singer: The Autobiography of Frank Mitchell, 1881–1967*, ed. Charlotte Frisbie and David McAllester. Tucson: University of Arizona Press.

Mitchell, Rose, and Charlotte Frisbie. 2001. *Tall Woman: The Life Story of Rose Mitchell, a Navajo Woman, c. 1874–1977*. Albuquerque: University of New Mexico Press.

Mithlo, Harry, and Conger Beasley Jr. 2020. *On Becoming Apache*. Lubbock: Texas Tech University Press.

Momaday, N. Scott. 2007. *Three Plays: The Indolent Boys, Children of the Sun, The Moon in Two Windows*. Norman: University of Oklahoma Press.

The Native American. 1909. January 1909.

Nequatewa, Edmund. 1993. *Born a Chief: The Nineteenth-Century Hopi Boyhood of Edmund Nequatewa*, ed. P. David Seaman. Tucson: University of Arizona Press.

Nevins, M. Eleanor. 2013. "'Grow with That, Walk with That': Hymes, Dialogicality, and Text Collections." *Journal of Folklore Research* 50: 79–116.

New York Times. 1912. December 15, 1912.
New York Times. 1922. October 6, 1922.
Nicholas, Dan. 193?. "Autobiography of Dan Nicholas," ed. Morris Opler. Morris Opler Papers, #14-25-3238, box 35, folder 15, and box 36, folder 1. Division of Rare and Manuscript Collections, Karl A. Kroch Library, Cornell University, Ithaca NY.
———. 1939. "Mescalero Apache Girl's Puberty Ceremony." *Palacio* 46: 203–4.
Occom, Samson. 1982 [1768]. "A Short Narrative of My Life." In Bernd Peyer, ed., *The Elders Wrote: An Anthology of Early Prose by North American Indians, 1768–1931*, 12–18. Berlin: Dietrich Riemer.
Opler, Morris. 1938. "A Chiricahua's Account of the Geronimo Campaign of 1886." *New Mexico Historical Review* 13: 360–86.
———. 1939. "A Description of a Tonkawa Peyote Meeting Held in 1902." *American Anthropologist* 41: 433–39.
———. 1941. *An Apache Lifeway: The Economic, Social, and Religious Institutions of the Chiricahua Indians*. Chicago: University of Chicago Press.
———. 2002 [1969]. *Apache Odyssey: A Journey Between Two Worlds*. Lincoln: University of Nebraska Press.
Parker, Arthur. 1915. "Editor's Comment." *American Indian Magazine* 3 (July–September, 1915): 3.
Parker, Robert Dale. 2011. *Changing Is Not Vanishing: A Collection of American Indian Poetry to 1930*. Philadelphia: University of Pennsylvania Press.
Perrett, Miriam. 2013. "Introduction" to Alicia Delgadillo, *From Fort Marion to Fort Sill*, xxi–xliii. Lincoln: University of Nebraska Press.
Powers-Beck, Jeffrey. 2004. *The American Indian Integration of Baseball*. Lincoln: University of Nebraska Press.
Pugsley, Andrea. 2003. "'As I kill this chicken so may I be punished if I tell an untruth': Chinese Opposition to Legal Discrimination in Arizona Territory." *Journal of Arizona History* 44: 171–190.
Quoyawayma, Polingaysi (Elizabeth White). 1977 [1964]. *No Turning Back: A Hopi Indian Woman's Struggle to Live in Two Worlds, as told to Vada Carlson*. Albuquerque: University of New Mexico Press.
Radin, Paul. 1913. "Personal Reminiscences of a Winnebago Indian." *Journal of American Folklore* 26: 293–318.
———. 1923. *The Winnebago Tribe. Thirty-seventh Annual Report of the Bureau of American Ethnology, for 1915–6*. Washington DC: Government Printing Office.
Radin, Paul, ed. 1999 [1926]. *Crashing Thunder: The Autobiography of an American Indian*. Ann Arbor: University of Michigan Press.

The Red Man. 1892. November-December 1892.

Reyhner, Jon, and Jeanne Elder. 2004. *American Indian Education: A History*. Norman: University of Oklahoma Press.

Riney, Scott. 1999. *The Rapid City Indian School: 1898–1933*. Norman: University of Oklahoma Press.

Robinson, Sherry. 2000. *Apache Voices: Their Stories of Survival as Told to Eve Ball*. Albuquerque: University of New Mexico Press.

Sapir, Edward. 1909. "Frances Johnson Is Cured by a Medicine Woman." *Takelma Texts, Anthropological Publications of the University of Pennsylvania Museum* 2: 184–89.

———. 1909. "A Personal Narrative of the Paiute War." In Sapir, *Wishram Texts. Publications of the American Ethnological Society* 2: 204–27.

Sapir, Edward, and Leslie Spier. 1930. *Wishram Ethnography. University of Washington Publications in Ethnography* 3: 222–23, 233–35.

Sekaquaptewa, Helen. 1993 [1969]. *Me and Mine: The Life Story of Helen Sekaquaptewa as told to Louise Udall*. Tucson: University of Arizona Press.

Shillinger, Sarah. 2008. *A Case Study of the American Indian Boarding School Movement: An Oral History of St. Joseph's Indian Industrial School*. Lewiston NY: Edwin Mellen.

Skinner, Woodward. 1987. *The Apache Rock Crumbles: The Captivity of Geronimo's People*. Pensacola FL: Skinner.

Sonnichsen, C. L. 1958. *The Mescalero Apaches*. Norman: University of Oklahoma Press.

Spindler, George. 1957. *Autobiographic Interviews of Eight Menomini Indian Males. Microcard Publications of Primary Records in Culture and Personality*. Ed. Bert Kaplan. II, no. 12, Madison WI: Microcard Foundation.

Spindler, Louise. 1957. *Sixty-one Rorschachs and Fifteen Expressive Autobiographic Interviews of Menomini Indian Women. Microcard Publications of Primary Records in Culture and Personality*. Ed. Bert Kaplan. II, no. 10, Madison WI: Microcard Foundation.

Stewart, Irene. 1980. *A Voice in Her Tribe: A Navajo Woman's Own Story*, ed. Doris Dawdy. Anthropological Papers no. 17. Socorro NM: Ballena.

Stockel, H. Henrietta. 2000. *Chiricahua Apache Women and Children: Safekeepers of the Heritage*. College Station: Texas A&M University Press.

Szasz, Margaret. 1999 [1974]. *Education and the American Indian: The Road to Self-Determination since 1928*, 3rd ed. Albuquerque: University of New Mexico Press.

Talayesva, Don. 1976 [1942]. *Sun Chief: The Autobiography of a Hopi Indian*, 2nd ed. Ed. Leo Simmons. New Haven: Yale University Press.

Thompson, Gerald. 1999. "Review of *The Chiricahua Apache Prisoners of War* by John Turcheneske, Jr." *American Historical Review* 104: 203–4.

Trafzer, Clifford, Matthew Sakiestewa Gilbert, and Loren Sisquoc, eds. 2012. *The Indian School on Magnolia Avenue*. Corvallis: Oregon State University Press.

Trafzer, Clifford, Jean Keller, and Lorene Sisquoc, eds. 2006. *Boarding School Blues: Revisiting American Indian Educational Experiences*. Lincoln: University of Nebraska Press.

Trennert, Robert Jr. 1988. *The Phoenix Indian School: Forced Assimilation in Arizona, 1891–1935*. Norman: University of Oklahoma Press.

Turcheneske, John, Jr. 1997. *The Chiricahua Apache Prisoners of War, 1896–1914*. Niwot: University Press of Colorado.

Tyler, Guy. 1960, 1963. Guy Tyler Collection of Mescalero Sound Recordings. Primary contributors Barney Naiche and Dan Nicholas. Collection no. LA218. Survey of California and Other Indian Languages, University of California, Berkeley. http://cla.berkeley.edu/collection/10185.

Vuckovic, Myriam. 2008. *Voices from Haskell: Indian Students between Two Worlds, 1884–1928*. Lawrence: University Press of Kansas.

Watt, Eva Tulene, as told to Keith H. Basso. 2004. *Don't Let the Sun Step Over You: A White Mountain Apache Family Life, 1860–1975*. Tucson: University of Arizona Press.

Webster, Anthony. 1999. "Sam Kenoi's Coyote Stories: Poetics and Rhetoric in Some Chiricahua Apache Narratives." *American Indian Culture and Research Journal* 23: 137–63.

———. 2012. "Samuel E. Kenoi's Portraits of White Men." In *Inside Dazzling Mountains: Southwest Native Verbal Arts*, ed. David Kozak, 175–94. Lincoln: University of Nebraska Press.

———. 2021. "Anthropology at the Water's Edge: Morris Opler Among the Apaches." *Journal of the Southwest* 63: 468–505.

———. 2021. Personal communication, November 12, 2021.

———. 2021. Personal communication, December 9, 2021.

Wetmore, Helen Cody. 1899. *Last of the Great Scouts: The Life Story of William F. Cody, "Buffalo Bill."* Duluth MN: Duluth Press.

Witmer, Linda. 2000. *The Indian Industrial School, Carlisle, Pennsylvania, 1879–1918*. Carlisle PA: Cumberland County Historical Society.

Wratten, Albert. 1986. "George Wratten: Friend of the Apaches." *Journal of Arizona History* 27: 91–124.

Yava, Albert. 1992 [1978]. *Big Falling Snow: A Tewa-Hopi Indian's Life and Times and the History and Traditions of His People*. Ed. Harold Courlander. Albuquerque: University of New Mexico Press.

Index

Page numbers in italics indicate illustrations

www.ingramcontent.com/pod-product-compliance
Lightning Source LLC
Chambersburg PA
CBHW060802310726
48980CB00002B/207

* 9 7 8 1 4 9 6 2 3 4 0 6 3 *